SEEKING BIGFOOT

SEEKING BIGFOOT

MICHAEL NEWTON

Schiffer Publishing Ltd®

4880 Lower Valley Road • Atglen, PA 19310

Other Schiffer Books by Michael Newton:

Strange West Virginia
Monsters
ISBN: 978-0-7643-4946-1

Strange California
Monsters
ISBN: 978-0-7643-3336-1

Strange Indiana Monsters
ISBN: 978-0-7643-2608-0

Strange Kentucky Monsters
ISBN: 978-0-7643-3440-5

Strange Monsters of the
Pacific Northwest
ISBN: 978-0-7643-3622-5

Strange Ohio Monsters
ISBN: 978-0-7643-4397-1

Strange Pennsylvania
Monsters
ISBN: 978-0-7643-3985-1

Copyright © 2015 by Michael Newton

Library of Congress Control Number: 2015938903

All rights reserved. No part of this work may be reproduced or used in any form or by any means—graphic, electronic, or mechanical, including photocopying or information storage and retrieval systems—without written permission from the publisher.

The scanning, uploading, and distribution of this book or any part thereof via the Internet or via any other means without the permission of the publisher is illegal and punishable by law. Please purchase only authorized editions and do not participate in or encourage the electronic piracy of copyrighted materials.

"Schiffer," "Schiffer Publishing, Ltd. & Design," and the "Design of pen and inkwell" are registered trademarks of Schiffer Publishing, Ltd.

Designed by Matt Goodman
Type set in Umbrage, Underwood Champion, Georgia & Benton

ISBN: 978-0-7643-4843-3
Printed in China

Published by Schiffer Publishing, Ltd.
4880 Lower Valley Road
Atglen, PA 19310
Phone: (610) 593-1777; Fax: (610) 593-2002
E-mail: Info@schifferbooks.com

For our complete selection of fine books on this and related subjects, please visit our website at www. schifferbooks.com. You may also write for a free catalog.

This book may be purchased from the publisher. Please try your bookstore first.

We are always looking for people to write books on new and related subjects. If you have an idea for a book, please contact us at proposals@schifferbooks.com.

Schiffer Publishing's titles are available at special discounts for bulk purchases for sales promotions or premiums. Special editions, including personalized covers, corporate imprints, and excerpts can be created in large quantities for special needs. For more information, contact the publisher.

EPIGRAPH

"You'll be amazed when I tell you that I'm sure that they exist."
—Dr. Jane Goodall
National Public Radio's *Science Friday* September 27, 2002

DEDICATION

For Dinah Roseberry

ACKNOWLEDGMENTS

I owe special thanks to Dinah Roseberry, friend and editor par excellence at Schiffer Books, for suggesting this work and for guiding it through production to become the tome you hold in your hands. Others offered help in securing illustrations, and four came through: thanks to Kaila Fisk, marketing and public relations associate with Jack Link's® Beef Jerky; to Dr. Jeffrey Meldrum at Idaho State University; and to two of the most persistent monster hunters in the business, Ken Gerhard and Nick Redfern, US field representatives of the Centre for Fortean Zoology. And once again, as always, thanks to Heather for sticking with me while I'm on the track of unknown creatures.

CONT

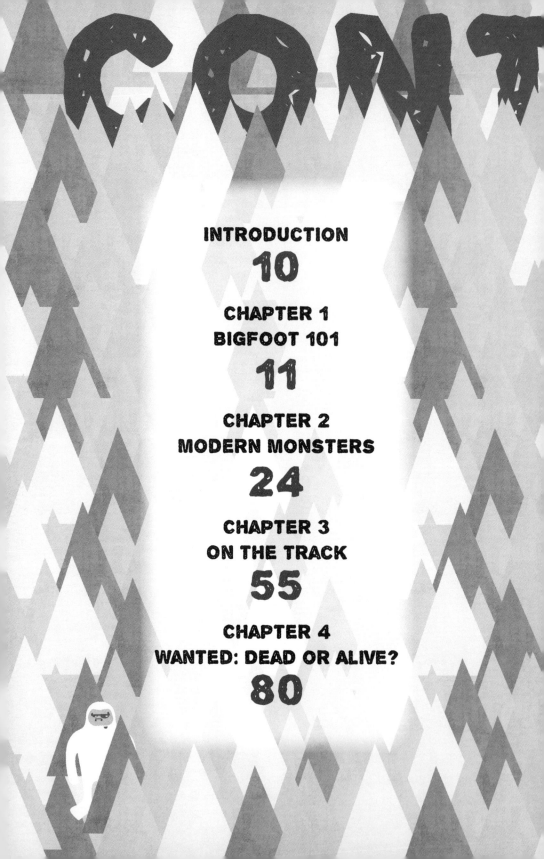

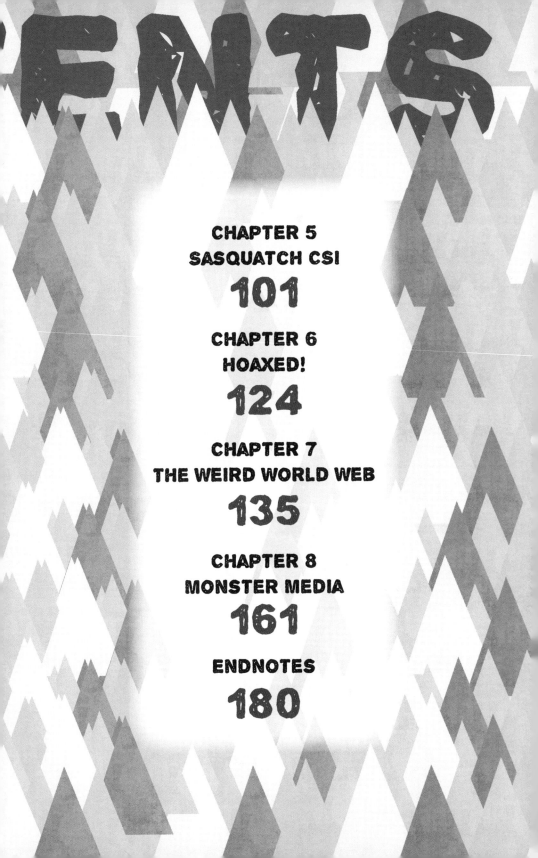

INTRODUCTION

Seeking Bigfoot chronicles the twenty-first-century North American search for "Big Hairy Monsters"—BHMs—variously known as Bigfoot, Sasquatch, Oh-Mah, Skookum, Momo, Skunk Ape, and by many other names. The subject of that quest, reported and pursued from time immemorial, is described as bipedal and covered with hair ranging in hue from white to black—and all shades in between. Witnesses sketch individual creatures in every size, from that of a human child to ten or twelve feet tall.

Bigfoot sightings have been reported from every US state except Hawaii, and from every Canadian province. The Pacific Northwest is often considered ground zero for sighting reports, but their distribution is remarkably broad. The Bigfoot Field Researchers Organization's (BFRO) archives include 266 modern reports from Florida, 248 from Illinois, 239 from Ohio, 200 from Texas, 178 from Michigan, 115 from Colorado, 113 from Missouri, and 100 each from New York and Pennsylvania. Even tiny Rhode Island has five Bigfoot sightings on file.[1]

Seeking Bigfoot presents data on the current study of Bigfoot in eight topical chapters.

- **Chapter 1** reviews nine classic cases that put Bigfoot "on the map" and established the riddle of its existence in public consciousness.
- **Chapter 2** relates sightings reported from forty-seven states and six Canadian provinces since 2000.
- **Chapter 3** introduces Bigfoot hunters and the methods employed in their ongoing quest.
- **Chapter 4** examines the heated debate as to whether Bigfoot should be killed to prove the species exists, or if conclusive evidence may be obtained by other means.
- **Chapter 5** details the physical evidence for Bigfoot's existence, ranging from huge footprints to microscopic DNA.
- **Chapter 6** highlights some well-known hoaxes in the field—and certain hoax reports that may, in fact, be fraudulent.
- **Chapter 7** lists and briefly evaluates Internet sources available for further study, as of press time for this volume.
- **Chapter 8** explores Bigfoot's portrayal in mass media, from television and the Internet to feature films and documentaries, including its impact on music and commercial advertising.

CHAPTER 1

BIGFOOT 101

Every story starts somewhere. For Bigfoot and his kin, the roots are global. Every culture, on every inhabited continent, has its own traditions of hairy, forest-dwelling giants who interact with humans as benefactors, predators, or cautious observers. In North America, when we advance beyond aboriginal lore, nine stories stand out as timeless classics. They include...

Early missionary
Elkanah Walker.
Credit: Author's collection.

Elkanah Walker's Letter: 1840

Missionary Elkanah Walker (1805–1877) crossed the Great Plains with bride Mary—billed as the "third woman to cross the Rockies"[1]—in 1838, spending the next nine years preaching to members of the Spokane tribe. In April 1840, Walker penned a letter to Rev. David Green, secretary for the American Board of Commissioners for Foreign Ministries, detailing various problems of frontier life, then closed with a startling report.

I suppose you will bear with me if I trouble you with a little of their superstition, which has recently come to my knowledge. They believe in the existence of a race of giants which inhabit a certain mountain off to the west of us. This mountain is covered with perpetual snow. They inhabit its top. They may be classed with Goldsmith's nocturnal class and they cannot see in the daytime. They hunt and do all of their work in the night. They are men stealers. They come to the people's lodges in the night when the people are asleep and take them, and put them under their skins and take them to their place of abode without even waking. When they wake in the morning they are wholly lost, not knowing in what direction their home is. The account that they give of these Giants will in some measure correspond with the Bible account of this race of beings. They say their track is about a foot and a half long. They will carry two or three beams upon their back at once. They frequently come in the night and steal their salmon from their nets and eat them raw. If the people are awake they always know when they are coming very near, by their strong smell, which is most intolerable. It is not uncommon for them to come in the night and give three whistles and then the stones will begin to hit their houses. The people believe that they are still troubled with their nocturnal visits.[2]

Walker's treatment of the "superstition" is ambiguous: dismissive on one hand, while linking it to scripture (which he accepted as literal truth) on the other. Religion aside, the giants' behavior and odor are staples of Bigfoot reports from earliest times to the present.

Bauman's Tale: 1893

Before he was a Rough Rider, police commissioner of New York City, governor of New York, or president of the United States, Theodore Roosevelt was a frontiersman, big-game hunter, and author. His third book, *The Wilderness Hunter* (1893), includes a story told to Roosevelt by a "grizzled, weather-beaten old mountain hunter" named Bauman who, as a young man—presumably in the 1840s or early 1850s—went trapping with an unnamed partner "among the mountains dividing the forks of the Salmon from the head of Wisdom River."[3] More specifically, those are the Bitterroot Mountains of eastern Idaho. The Wisdom River is, today, the Big Hole River.

Theodore Roosevelt, author of *The Wilderness Hunter* and later President of the United States.
Credit: Library of Congress.

As Roosevelt explains, the region "had an evil reputation because, the year before, a solitary hunter who had wandered into it was slain, seemingly by a wild beast, the half-eaten remains found afterwards by some mining prospectors who had passed his camp only the night before." Undismayed, Bauman and his partner pitched camp and laid their trap lines for beaver, returning near dusk to find that "something, apparently a bear, had visited camp, and had rummaged about among their things, scattering the contents of their packs and, in sheer wantonness, destroyed their lean-to. The footprints of the beast were quite plain, but at first they paid no particular heed to them, busying themselves with rebuilding the lean-to, laying out their beds and stores and lighting the fire."

Only after supper did they examine the tracks more closely, whereupon Bauman's partner remarked, "That bear has been walking on two legs."[4]

Bauman laughed it off, but got a shock at midnight, when he woke to strange sounds. As related by Roosevelt, "[H]is nostrils were struck by a strong, wild-beast odor, and he caught the loom of a great body in the darkness at the mouth of the lean-to. Grasping his rifle, he fired at the vague, threatening shadow, but must have missed, for immediately afterwards he heard the smashing of the under wood as the thing, whatever it was, rushed off into the impenetrable blackness of the forest and the night."[5]

Sleepless till dawn, Bauman and friend resumed their trapping—and returned at day's end to find their camp trashed again. Roosevelt writes: "The visitor of the preceding day had returned, and in wanton malice, had tossed about their camp kit and bedding, and destroyed the shanty. The ground was marked up by its tracks, and on leaving the camp it had gone along the soft earth by the brook. The footprints were as plain as if on snow, and, after a careful scrutiny of the trail, it certainly did seem as if, whatever the thing was, it had walked off on but two legs."[6] A roaring fire kept the prowler at bay overnight, and the trappers agreed to leave the next afternoon after checking their traps one last time.

The next morning passed without incident, until Bauman and his partner split up, Bauman going to retrieve a final string of traps, while his partner packed up their camp. After securing three more pelts, Bauman returned to camp and found a ghastly scene.

At first Bauman could see nobody; nor did he receive an answer to his call. Stepping forward he again shouted, and as he did so his eye fell on the body of his friend, stretched beside the trunk of a great fallen spruce. Rushing towards it the horrified trapper found that the body was still warm, but that the neck was broken, while there were four great fang marks in the throat.

The footprints of the unknown beast-creature, printed deep in the soft soil, told the whole story.

The unfortunate man, having finished his packing, had sat down on the spruce log with his face to the fire, and his back to the dense woods, to wait for his companion. While thus waiting, his monstrous assailant, which must have been lurking in the woods, waiting for a chance to catch one of the adventurers unprepared, came silently up from behind, walking with long noiseless steps and seemingly still on two legs. Evidently unheard, it reached the man, and broke his neck by wrenching his head back with its fore paws, while it buried its teeth in his throat. It had not eaten the body, but apparently had romped and gamboled around it in uncouth, ferocious glee, occasionally rolling over and over it; and had then fled back into the soundless depths of the woods.[7]

Bauman immediately fled, with nothing but his horse and rifle, riding through the night until he was beyond the stalking predator's reach.

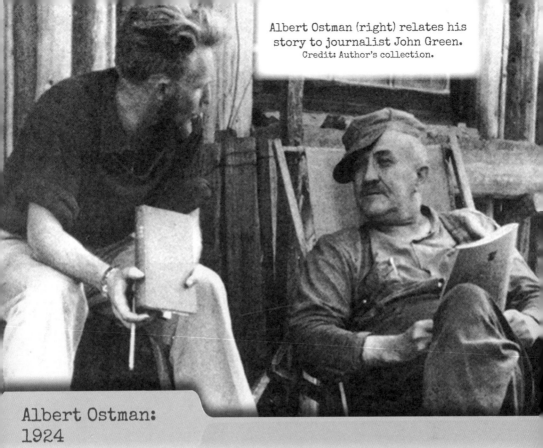

Albert Ostman: 1924

Canadian logger Albert Ostman (1893–1975) tried his hand at prospecting for gold in the summer of 1924, camping at the head of British Columbia's Toba Inlet. On his fifth night alone, nocturnal prowlers began tampering with Ostman's gear and rifling his pack while he slept. On the eighth night, something scooped him up inside his sleeping bag and carried him away. After hours in stifling darkness, his abductor dropped the sleeping bag and Ostman heard "chatter—some kind of talk I did not understand." Emerging, he confronted four hairy bipeds that "look[ed] like a family, old man, old lady and two young ones, a boy and a girl. The boy and the girl seemed to be scared of me. The old lady did not seem too pleased about what the old man had dragged home. But the old man was waving his arms and telling them all what he had in mind."[8]

After three days in captivity unharmed, Ostman escaped by feeding the "old man" a can of snuff, then firing a rifle shot to frighten the others and fleeing on foot. Fearing ridicule or worse, he kept the story to himself until 1957, when he told it to Canadian researcher John Green. Green was skeptical, noting behavioral and geographical discrepancies when he recounted Ostman's story in 1978.[9]

Police magistrate A. M. Naismith held a different view, after interviewing Ostman on August 20, 1957. According to Naismith's affidavit, "I found Mr. Ostman to be a man of sixty-four years of age, in full possession of his mental faculties. Of pleasant manner and with a good sense of humor. I questioned

Mr. Ostman thoroughly in reference to the story given by Mr. Green. I cross-examined him and used every means to endeavor to find a flaw in either his personality or his story, but could find neither." Ostman also signed a solemn declaration, under oath, attesting to the truth of his story.[10]

Ape Canyon: 1924

Around the same time Ostman met his Bigfoot family, in July 1924, a group of miners allegedly fought a pitched battle with shaggy monsters near Mount St. Helens, Washington, at a site known today as Ape Canyon. Fred Beck told the story forty-three years later in a self-published booklet titled *I Fought the Apemen of Mount St. Helens, Wa.* (1967). As with Ostman's tale of kidnapping, Beck's story remains controversial today, truncated by some to make it more believable, tainted in the eyes of skeptics by the possible involvement of a notorious hoaxer.

Briefly stated, Beck and his companions were spending their sixth year prospecting for gold, occasionally troubled by huge footprints in the neighborhood, accompanied by shrill whistling and "a booming, thumping sound—just like something was hitting its self [*sic*] on its chest." While fetching water, Beck and one of his friends saw a seven-foot, blackish-brown Bigfoot, and fired several shots to hold it at bay. Around midnight, several creatures attacked the miners' cabin, hurling boulders, while Beck and company fired blindly through the door and roof. The battle raged until dawn, when the miners emerged, saw one creature standing on a nearby ridge, and blasted it into a gorge some 400 feet deep.[11]

Fred Beck with the rifle he allegedly used to fight "psychic" apemen in 1924. Credit: Author's collection.

Fact or fantasy? John Green believed the story, writing in 1978: "Did this really happen? I think so...There isn't a shadow of a suggestion as to why they would make up such a story and keep telling it all their lives."[12]

Against that view stands Beck's own published story, rife with claims of mysticism and the paranormal, urging readers toward "a spiritual and metaphysical understanding of the case." Beck experienced "visions" from childhood onward and, after 1924, "spent many years in healing work." He and his partners were directed to their claim by "a spiritual being, a large Indian dressed in buckskin," and the apes who stormed his cabin also bore "a direct association with the psychic realm."[13] He wrote:

I hope this book does not discourage too much those interested souls who are looking and trying to solve the mystery of the abominable snowmen. If someone captured one, I would have to swallow most of the content of this book, for I am about to make a bold statement: No one will ever capture one, and no one will ever kill one—in other words, present to the world a living one in a cage, or find a dead body of one to be examined by science. I know there are stories that some have been captured but got away. So will they always get away.[14]

A further complication involves self-proclaimed prankster Rant Mullens, who claimed (in 1982) that he and his uncle, George Ross, rolled the boulders onto Beck's cabin in 1924. Later, while working for the US Forest Service in 1930, Mullens allegedly carved a pair of wooden feet, seventeen inches long, using them to plant tracks around Mount St. Helens. By 1969, when he reportedly sold a pair of "feet" to fellow hoaxer Ray Wallace, Mullens allegedly had eight pairs in various sizes, laying trails at random for his personal amusement.[15]

So, was Beck deluded or deceived by Mullens? Did Mullens—an admitted hoaxer—simply lie to get attention during his declining years? Was John Green right in trusting Beck's account? The muddled mystery is likely to remain unsolved.

Muchalat Harry: 1928

Another tale of kidnapping by Bigfoot comes to us from Peter Byrne, immersed in searching for Bigfoot-type creatures worldwide since 1948. Along the way, he met Father Anthony Terhaar of Mount Angel Abbey in St. Benedict, Oregon, who recounted events allegedly occurring on Vancouver Island in 1928.

The principal, a Nootka tribesman named Muchalat Harry, was trapping in late autumn when, like Albert Ostman four years earlier, he was snatched from fireside in his sleep and carried off to "a sort of camp" occupied by a score of apelike creatures.[16] Harry initially feared that the beasts would eat him, but they left him unharmed and soon seemed to lose interest, permitting him to escape and reach his home village, some forty-five miles distant. Father Terhaar, a rural missionary in those days, helped nurse him back to health, reporting that Harry's hair turned pure white over the course of three weeks' convalescence.

Byrne reserved judgment on Harry's tale, but noted Father Terhaar's observation that Harry never retrieved his lost traps, and refused to reenter the woods for the rest of his life.

Ruby Creek: 1941

Our next "classic" case comes from Ruby Creek, British Columbia, thirty miles up the Fraser River from Agassiz. In September 1941, First Nations members George and Jeannie Chapman occupied a cabin there, with their three children. On the afternoon in question, the eldest son told Mrs. Chapman that a cow was approaching the homestead. A closer look revealed that the "cow" was, in fact, "a gigantic man covered with hair, not fur. The hair seemed to be about four inches long all over, and of a pale yellow-brown color." Mrs. Chapman left the cabin with her children—George was at work—and fled downstream to a nearby village. She later described the beast to author Ivan Sanderson as 7½ feet tall, with a small head, no visible neck, an "immensely thick" chest, and long arms. Its bare face and hands appeared black, in contrast to its lighter-colored coat of hair.[17]

The Chapman home at Ruby Creek, as it appeared in 1941. Credit: Author's collection.

George returned home to find his cabin empty and an outbuilding ransacked, its door smashed in with long brown hairs stuck to the lintel, and a fifty-five-gallon barrel of salt fish dragged outside, its contents scattered around the yard. He saw the creature's huge footprints trailing his family's tracks toward the river, and determined that Jeannie had escaped with the children. Every morning for the next week, Chapman left the house to find fresh footprints in the yard, but no more damage was inflicted on the property. Mrs. Chapman told Sanderson that the beast made "an awful funny noise," mimicked by her husband with "exactly the same strange, gurgling whistle" that Sanderson heard from other Bigfoot witnesses.[18]

Sanderson concluded: "I absolutely refuse to listen to anybody who might say they were lying. Admittedly, honest men are such a rarity as possibly to be non-existent, but I have met a few who could qualify and I put the Chapmans near the head of the list."[19]

William Roe: 1955

In October 1955, William Roe met a Bigfoot while hunting near Tete Jaune Cache, a small town in British Columbia, located eighty miles west of Jasper, Alberta. As described in a sworn affidavit dated August 26, 1957, he first mistook the creature for a bear, then realized his error when it stood upright. According to Roe's statement:

My first impression was of a huge man, about six feet tall, almost three feet wide, and probably weighing somewhere near three hundred pounds. It was covered from head to foot with dark brown silver-tipped hair. But as it came closer I saw by its breasts that it was female.

And yet, its torso was not curved like a female's. Its broad frame was straight from shoulder to hip. Its arms were much thicker than a man's arms, and longer, reaching almost to its knees. Its feet were broader proportionately than a man's, about five inches wide at the front and tapering to much thinner heels. When it walked it placed the heel of its foot down first, and I could see the grey-brown skin or hide on the soles of its feet.[20]

Next, Roe suspected a film crew at work, but he saw no cameras and decided "it would be impossible to fake such a specimen." Soon, the creature caught his scent and "looked directly at me through an opening in the brush. A look of amazement crossed its face. It looked so comical at the moment I had to grin... The thought came to me that if I shot it, I would possibly have a specimen of great interest to scientists the world over...I leveled my rifle. The creature was still walking rapidly away, again turning its head to look in my direction. I lowered the rifle. Although I have called the creature 'it,' I felt now that it was a human being and I knew I would never forgive myself if I killed it."[21]

Before departing, Roe found piles of feces "in five different places, and although I examined it thoroughly, could find no hair or shells of bugs or insects. So I believe it was strictly a vegetarian."[22]

Ivan Sanderson took Roe's report at face value, describing it as a "priceless document."[23]

Bluff Creek: 1958

In May 1958, a construction crew led by Raymond Wallace began work on the Klamath River Highway, otherwise known as California State Route 96. By August they had reached Bluff Creek, twenty-eight miles north of Willow Creek and fifty-four miles south of Happy Camp. The work was slow, and it soon took a detour into the strange.

According to the stories published then and for years thereafter, tractor operator Gerald Crew reported for work on August 27 and found his vehicle surrounded by sixteen-inch bare footprints. He followed them over rugged terrain, up and down sheer slopes, measuring a stride that ranged from forty-six to sixty inches between footprints. A month passed before the tracks reappeared, and in mid-September a crewman's wife wrote to Eureka's *Humboldt Times*, reporting stories of a "wild man" in the area.[24]

Times columnist Andrew Genzoli printed the letter and, as Ivan Sanderson later wrote, "the balloon went up."[25] Crew delivered plaster casts of the footprints on October 4, reporting that his fellow workers called the unseen prowler "Big Foot." Genzoli ran a front-page photo of the casts and wrote, "There is a mystery in the mountains of northeastern Humboldt County, waiting for a solution... Who is making the huge sixteen-inch tracks in the vicinity of Bluff Creek? Are the tracks a human hoax? Or, are they actual marks of a huge but harmless wild-man, traveling through the wilderness? Can this be some legendary-sized animal?"[26]

The ink was barely dry on that editorial when Wilbur Wallace—Raymond's brother and a member of the road crew—reported even more startling news.

Ray Wallace (left) threatens legal action over claims that he faked Bigfoot tracks like the one shown at right. Credit: Author's collection.

Someone or something with huge feet, he said, had carried a fifty-five-gallon drum of diesel fuel 175 feet from the construction site and tossed it into a gorge. The same burly vandal had taken an eighteen-inch culvert pipe and tossed it down another slope, before rolling a 250-pound earthmover's tire a quarter-mile from the work site and pitching it into a deep ravine. Ray Wallace, described by Sanderson as "a hard-boiled and pragmatic man," declared himself "skeptical."[27]

Or was he?

Officers of the Humboldt County Sheriff's Office suspected Raymond himself of faking the tracks, prompting a furious response. "I'm not going in," Wallace told the *Times*. "If they want to put out a warrant I'm going to sue them for slander—and I won't fool around about it! If they think they're going to make a laughing stock out of me, they've got another thing coming."[28]

Times reporter Bill Chambers reported those comments, then wrote on October 15 that "Bigfoot has been seen" by two witnesses described as "husky construction workers with good eyesight."[28]

Perhaps. And yet, after Ray Wallace died at a Centralia, Washington, nursing home in November 2002, Ray's son Michael told any reporter who would listen that his father had faked the Bluff Creek footprints, along with countless others, adding bogus hair and feces samples to the list, even claiming credit for the most famous purported Bigfoot film of all time. When that news broke, a writer for the *Eureka Times-Standard* called June Beal, widow of late *Times* editor

L. W. "Scoop" Beal, to get her take on the story. "They were in on this hoax," she said of her husband and Wallace. "It was just a fun thing and the fun got out of hand."[29]

And yet, there were discrepancies within the exposé itself. Aside from the peril of taking an admitted liar's word for anything, it was patently impossible for Wallace to have faked all Bigfoot tracks and sightings logged from coast to coast, in every state, starting a century or more before his birth in 1918.

As John Driscoll wrote in the *Times-Standard*, "This goes back to the rule for misinformation and general trickery: Just because you made it up, doesn't mean it isn't true."[30]

Roger Patterson: 1967

Ex-rodeo cowboy Roger Patterson (1926-1972) was fascinated by coverage of the Bluff Creek tracks, devoting the rest of his life to the search for Bigfoot. In 1966, he published a compilation of reports titled *Do Abominable Snowmen of America Really Exist?* and the following year he produced what some investigators still believe to be the most important piece of evidence as yet obtained for large, unclassified primates in North America. Skeptics dismiss that evidence as an obvious, even malicious, hoax.

After publishing his book, Patterson hoped to produce a film about Bigfoot with friend Robert Gimlin, embarking on research excursions to seek evidence or a glimpse of the creature itself. On October 20, 1967, the hunters reportedly got lucky, capturing fifty-three seconds of 16-mm film depicting an apparent, obviously female BHM. Losing both their quarry and their horses in the heat of the moment, Patterson and Gimlin regrouped to track the creature for three miles, before losing its trail in heavy brush. Along the way, they made plaster casts of two footprints, one left and one right, and covered others to protect them from the elements. Forestry worker Lyle Laverty photographed those prints on October 21, and taxidermist/outdoorsman Robert Titmus arrived on October 30, making more casts and trying to plot the creature's movements on a map.

Then began the process of soliciting expert opinions on the film's authenticity, a subject that still sparks acrimonious, sometimes slanderous, debate. Various anthropologists, zoologists, anatomists, and special effects experts have weighed in on the subject since 1967. Professional debunkers have proposed at least three candidates, including the wife of hoaxer Ray Wallace as Patterson's "man in the ape suit," but none yet have produced conclusive evidence of fraud. Some Hollywood "insiders" claimed that makeup artist John Chambers made the hypothetical costume, an assertion denied by Chambers himself, shortly before his death in 2001. Another costume maker, Phillip Morris, says he sold Patterson

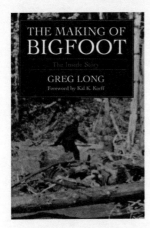

a gorilla suit in 1967, but comparison of his standard work with the creature on film reveals glaring discrepancies, blamed by Morris on radical aftermarket modifications.

The net result: a snarl of accusations and rebuttals, calm analyses, and heated arguments that sometimes verge upon hysteria. Even within the camp of "Bigfoot believers," opinions on Patterson's film are starkly divided. Nothing has changed in that regard since 1967.

And the search goes on.

Greg Long's *The Making of Bigfoot* claimed—but failed to prove—that the Patterson film is fraudulent. Credit: Author's collection.

CHAPTER 2

MODERN MONSTERS

Where should we look for Bigfoot? Anywhere and everywhere, according to reports on file with groups devoted to the search. That much was known by 1961, when Ivan Sanderson published his classic work *Abominable Snowmen: Legend Come to Life*, and John Green reinforced the message seventeen years later in *Sasquatch: The Apes Among Us*. In 1993, Rick Berry's *Bigfoot on the East Coast* presented an astounding list of BHM sightings far removed from the creature's traditional Pacific Northwest stomping ground. Today, Bigfoot reports from far and wide are detailed in a score of books devoted to individual states, and that number grows yearly. The forty-seven states with twenty-first-century sightings on file (so far) include:

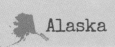 Virginia

Old Dominion witnesses have logged sixty-three Bigfoot sightings since 1970. Around 2:30 p.m. on October 14, 2011, a group of Florida tourists was camped in Grayson Highlands State Park near Mouth of Wilson, a small town in the Appalachian Mountains. The party included three couples and four children, all of whom observed "a large hair-covered figure" moving through the trees some 200 yards distant. Despite their remove from the figure, the witnesses described it in remarkable detail: over seven feet tall, weighing 350 to 400 pounds with an "athletic" build, covered in black hair two to three inches long, with forearms that "seemed long for the body." Two of the campers snapped photos of the creature, whatever it was, and one is posted on the BFRO's website.[1]

Around 4 a.m. on April 3, 2014, a man driving to work on U.S. Route 11 near Woodstock (Shenandoah County) saw "a tall dark figure" cross the road "in two large bounds" and disappear in roadside brush. Slowing, with his windows down, he "heard nothing, no limbs breaking, no ground noises. It was very strange." Judging from a nearby stop sign, he pegged the creature's height at 7½ feet. (BFRO Report #45570)

Alaska

The Last Frontier claims twenty-three reports since 1985. In July 2009, Bigfoot visited a residential neighborhood in Fairbanks, roughly one mile from that city's University of Alaska campus. A motorist on Auburn Drive, passing Pearl Creek Elementary School and its locally famous garden at 6 p.m., saw the reddish-haired creature standing at roadside. It bolted for the woods as the gap between them closed to fifty yards, then the driver stopped and watched it flee with a "hoppy kind of run," clearly distinguished from a limp.

The creature, he said, was roughly six feet tall and weighed about 200 pounds. Curiosity piqued, he questioned other locals, learning that several Pearl Creek students had seen the creature pass their school a week before his own sighting. His conclusion: "It was either real or there was a man in a VERY, VERY convincing costume."[2]

Alabama

The Cotton State has eighty-three Bigfoot reports on file, dating from 1979. At 6 p.m. on March 12, 2010, while driving home from a shopping errand in Kansas (Walker County), Alabama, a female motorist saw "something white squatting down on the side of the highway," thirty to forty yards ahead of her car. As she approached, it "stood straight up and turned around slowly and walked into the woods real calm." Erect, the creature was taller than a nearby street sign and was covered in "dirty white fur." Other local witnesses, including two from the woman's immediate family, claimed sightings of white and black BHMs dating back to the 1990s. A follow-up investigation by BFRO member Kevin Smykal revealed three nights of "frenzied" barking by neighborhood dogs, on four nights surrounding the woman's encounter. Strange vocalizations described as "a very deep, powerful, echoing scream or holler" were also reported.[3]

On October 2, 2013, a nocturnal fisherman heard and saw "two large, brown, hairy-looking cavemen-looking things" fighting in a creek near Bayview Lake, north of Birmingham. Both fled in haste from his flashlight beam. (BFRO Report #43689)

On June 8, 2014, a driver approaching Bremen (Cullman County) on State Route 69 saw a deer cross the road, pursued by a brownish-black biped seven to eight feet tall, with a "huge upper body, sorta narrow at the hips." (BFRO Report #45296)

Nine days later, on June 17, another motorist met Bigfoot on State Route 9 near Cedar Bluff (Cherokee County). The beast was seven to eight feet tall and covered in dark hair. She later told the BFRO, "It stood and stared at me a few seconds and then turned and walked back into the woods. It took two strides and it was gone. I was freaked out!" (BFRO Report #45464)

Around 3:30 a.m. on September 14, 2014, a family of four was returning from a visit to relatives on County Road 73 west of Newville (Henry County). Three passengers were sleeping when the driver saw "a very broad creature that stood on two legs," later telling her husband that "what stuck out to her the most was the figure's cone-shaped head and the way the hair shined when the lights hit it." (BFRO Report #46746)

Arizona's monster-haunted Mogollon Rim. Credit: US National Park Service.

Arizona

The arid Southwest may seem unlikely turf for forest-dwelling giants, but Bigfoot makes itself known in the region nonetheless, with seventy-six Arizona reports since 1975. On May 29, 2010, around 6 p.m., while camping near Forest Road 115 north of the Mogollon Rim (Coconino County), a man and his son saw a figure resembling "a VERY large man in a ghillie suit walk across the opening in the trees to my left." It walked "rather casually (kinda slow), but it covered a lot of ground in very few steps." Subsequent interrogation of the witnesses convinced BFRO investigator "Sandra M." that there may have been two creatures near the campsite, one brown with lighter patches, the second nearly black. In retrospect, the campers recalled prior incidents at the same location, wherein they were pelted with stones, saw "eyeshine" near their campfire, and heard "howls and tree knocks" from the surrounding woods.[4]

A poster for the film that made the Fouke Monster one of America's most famous cryptids. Credit: Author's collection.

With eighty-four sightings on record, residents of the Razorback State were familiar with Bigfoot long before Charles Pierce produced his now-classic film *The Legend of Boggy Creek* in 1972. Forty years later—at 4 a.m. on September 13, 2012—a woman driving near Fouke, on Miller County Road 10, saw a tall, hairy biped cross fifty feet in front of her car. It walked with "long but unhurried strides, then stepped over a barbed wire fence" and vanished into roadside woods. Questioned two months later by BFRO member Tal Branco, the witness described her Bigfoot as "a good eight feet tall," its torso "big and thick" but "not fat," supported on "very long and muscular legs." Its hair was long, dark brown with lighter patches, and its sex was indeterminate. For a "split second," its left eye reflected "a distinct red glow" from the woman's headlights. Branco deemed the witness "a credible observer."[5]

 California

Ten days after the aforementioned Arkansas sighting, on September 23, 2012, a deer hunter saw Bigfoot in the Sierra Nevada Mountains, west of Markleeville (Alpine County). He described it to the BFRO as "a bipedal primate about eight feet tall," with a wide muscular torso and a brow that "was extremely pronounced, its forehead was small with the back of its head slightly pointed." Its arms were "extremely long, hairy, lean yet muscular," ending in hands with "very long palms and long fingers." After staring at the witness for a moment, the creature "sprinted up the hill and vanished behind the trees faster than a deer bolts into a dead run from a standstill." Forest shade prevented the hunter from judging whether the thing's hair was black or dark brown. Nearby, the hunter found a mutilated deer carcass, "probably killed a few weeks prior." That night, the witness and two companions heard "cracking sounds of timber, then a huge tree by our camp come crashing down." BFRO investigator Tom Yamarone found the hunter "sincere and very detailed in his recounting" of the incident.[6]

Colorado

O ur next report comes from the neighborhood of Bailey, Colorado, southwest of Denver in Pike National Forest, near Highway 285. At 7:45 p.m. on May 29, 2012, two women were returning from a woodland hike to Bailey Lodge, located 2½ miles southwest of town, when a "huge grayish" figure ran past them "at a speed so fast that at first they couldn't imagine what it would be." The runner was "human looking," but "seemed to be a lot taller than them." When questioned by BFRO member Mark Taylor, both witnesses— dubbed "W1" and "W2"—"solidly agreed that the subject was estimated at seven to eight feet tall, bulky, covered in dark gray to black hair (not clothing)." While humanoid in form, the creature's mode of running was "slightly 'off' or 'peculiar' when compared to humans but smooth and graceful." Taylor judged "W1" to be a "solid, straightforward person.[7]

One Sunday in March 2014, two friends returning from a trip to Conifer glimpsed Bigfoot in Jefferson County, between Wellington Lake and Long Scraggy Mountain Ranch. They say it "effortlessly" crossed the road, 400 to 500 feet in front of their car, walking upright with "a few long strides." Distance precluded any further details. (BFRO Report #45666)

Delaware

F ar to the east, our next witness met Bigfoot at 8:55 p.m. on January 13, 2004, after a night class at Delaware Technical Community College in Georgetown, bound for home in nearby Laurel. Traveling back roads to save time, the witness rounded a curve and saw a large figure standing beside a utility pole, its back turned toward oncoming headlights. The creature was seven to eight feet tall (judged by comparison to the utility pole), had broad shoulders and, except for its hands, was covered in thick black hair. When the biped turned to look at him, the witness "peeled out" and sped for home.[8]

Florida

Florida's Bigfoot is commonly known as the Swamp Ape—or Skunk Ape, based on its foul aroma. A recent sighting occurred near Bristol, in Liberty County, around dusk on March 28, 2013. While driving through Torreya State Park on County Road 270, a motorist slammed on his brakes to avoid hitting a "huge tall black creature" that crossed the road in four strides and was gone. Based on that fleeting glimpse, the witness judged the creature to be "at least" nine feet tall and four feet wide. Shocked and frightened, he rushed to the home of his sister-in-law, and they went back together, surprised to find that the beast had returned. Speaking to BFRO investigator David Bakara on April 2, the female witness described the creature as "four times the size" of her 300-pound husband.[9]

Iowa

owa residents have filed sixty Bigfoot reports since 1970. Around 5:15 p.m. on August 31, 2011, the latest witness was driving home from work in Rickardsville, passing Sageville on Highway 52 en route to Dubuque. The region's normal wildlife consists of deer, coyotes, and an occasional fox, but on this day the driver saw "a dark figure in a forward lunging position running [and] at the same time leap over the guard cable" at roadside. Writing to the BFRO's website on September 1, he said, "I could clearly see its dark shorter hair and its shoulder and upper arm as if being lifted to clear the thick bushes." He pegged the creature's height at six feet, with a "well built upper body and very thick muscular legs. Its head was long and cone shaped. It looked to weigh around 300 pounds or so." BFRO investigator Steve Moon interviewed the witness twice, judging him to be "extremely credible and a very astute observer."[10]

 Idaho

he Gem State claims sixty-nine reports since 1963. On June 5, 2011, around 4 p.m., a husband and wife met Bigfoot while riding all-terrain vehicles along the Payette River, sixteen miles from Crouch and three to four miles from the Silver Creek Plunge Resort, in the Boise National Forest. The female witness described "a huge dark figure on two legs, upright bounding right up the mountainside to my right." Her husband recalled it as "huge, hairy and fast." Elaborating for BFRO investigator Todd Strong, they depicted the Bigfoot as "muscular with long hair that was dark brown, to the point of almost being black." Strong deemed their testimony "reliable."[11]

Idaho's Payette River. Credit: US National Park Service.

Illinois

With 248 reports on file since 1964, the Land of Lincoln is no stranger to BHM sightings. At 11:05 p.m. on March 4, 2013, on Illinois Route 29 near Edinburg, in Christian County, a young female motorist paused at a T-intersection's stop sign, saw several deer bounding across an open field in front of her, pursued into the woods by a large, "very, very hairy" creature running on two legs. After hearing her story, the girl's parents questioned relatives and neighbors about similar occurrences, learning that a "juvenile" Bigfoot had been seen around Clarksdale, sixteen miles from the site of their daughter's encounter, over the past year. The creature glimpsed in March was "over seven feet tall" and "very chunky," covered in brown hair.[12]

Around dusk on July 12, 2014, a Galesburg teacher saw Bigfoot cross Illinois Route 164 west of town, near the boundary separating Knox and Warren Counties. He described the creature as "very dark and hairy, it was running on all fours, yet it was very tall. Its rear end was up higher than its front end and it appeared to have no muzzle. Its face was flat...Its front legs moved as if a human would be leaning over a tricycle peddling, and its back legs moved with a human running motion, including what appeared to be knees." (BFRO Report #47249)

Three months later, on October 10, a hiker in Buffalo Rock State Park (La Salle County) heard crashing in the brush as he stood atop the Frog Effigy, a 340-foot-long tumulus erected by ancient Native American mound builders. As he told the BFRO, "I did not smell it or see its face. I only heard it and saw it from the side and back." (BFRO Report #46878)

Finally, on December 6, 2014, a deer hunter saw two hairy bipeds, one gray and one "dark black," in separate encounters near Findlay (Shelby County). He snapped "a series of pics that aren't the best, but show a dark figure walking away," one of which appears on the BFRO's website. (BFRO Report #47403)

Indiana

The Hoosier State has seventy-four Bigfoot reports on file since 1975. On January 16, 2014, a hunter from Martinsville saw a "large shaggy hairy thing" squatting beside the White River. At his approach, it made a "humph" sound, rose, and "moved off down river as if it wasn't worried about me." The witness described it as seven to eight feet tall, covered in "dirty brownish red hair," with the "build of a professional body builder except its arms was longer than ours. It also appeared to have a slouch as it stood up."[13]

Kansas

Most Americans who picture Kansas think of wheat fields, flat terrain, and Old West cattle drives. Bigfoot rarely enters the equation, but the Sunflower State claims at least thirty-eight sightings since September 1886, when the *New York Times* reported the capture of a shaggy "wild family" in Washington County.[14] More recently, at 1:30 p.m. on June 19, 2012, a family driving on US Highway 54, near Pratt, saw a hairy biped "maybe nine or ten feet tall" standing at roadside. As they approached, it ran away at a "leisurely gait," taking five-or six-foot strides. In conversation with BFRO member Carter Buschardt, the male witness reported seeing the same or a similar creature near dusk, around June 12, a mile from the site of the later encounter. The first Bigfoot, he said, had carried a deer's carcass over its shoulder. Another deer, perhaps hit by a car, was sprawled near the scene of the second sighting. In each case, the creature's dark brown hair had gray highlights, as if from age.[15]

On the evening of November 14, 2014, a married couple and the husband's brother were returning from Hays to their rural Rooks County home on 10 Road, when the woman noted "two red eyes staring at us" from woods to the west. Both men saw "something that could have been either white or light gray" moving through the forest, then spied "another set of red eyes" east of the highway, elevated eight to nine feet above ground. (BFRO Report #47267)

 Kentucky

Kentucky boasts ninety-eight Bigfoot reports since 1950. While setting trail cameras on family property near Wallins (Harlan County), a teenage witness reportedly met Bigfoot at 6:30 p.m. on January 10, 2013. Seen from a range of thirty feet, the creature was covered in grayish-brown hair "like sloth fur," which "looked wet," and it proved "very mobile" when running away. It left behind "a faint musky smell." Returning to the site a day later, the witness measured a nearby tree and determined the biped must have been seven feet tall.[16]

 Louisiana

The Pelican State has produced at least forty Bigfoot reports since 1971. At 9:30 a.m. on December 10, 2005, a hunter logged the latest sighting near Goldonna, in the Kisatchie National Forest (Natchitoches Parish). At first, he thought the passing figure was "a very large man," but a second hard look revealed a mostly black biped whose hair "was white from the ground up on each leg" for twelve to twenty inches above ground. By comparison to nearby trees, he judged the beast was nine to ten feet tall, with long arms and legs. BFRO investigator Kevin Smykal suggests that lighter coloration on the shins may be explained by sand stuck to the creature's hair.[17]

Kisatchie National Forest, Louisiana.
Credit: US National Park Service.

Minnesota

The Land of 10,000 Lakes claims fifty-five Bigfoot sightings since 1972. Around 9 a.m. on April 20, 2010, a motorist driving near Cloquet (Carlton County) reportedly saw "a dark animal" sitting beside railroad tracks, "about a thousand feet" from the man's car. That distance seems extreme for a witness described as "elderly" on the BFRO's website, but his depiction of the event is fairly detailed. He saw the creature rising "like a man," standing erect at over six feet tall, heavily built and covered with black hair that was "long down the back." After ten minutes or so, it walked into the nearby woods, leaving its observer convinced that the creature "was not a man and not a bear." BFRO member "Andy P." deemed the aged witness "very credible and honest."[18]

Missouri

The Show-Me State has a long tradition of Bigfoot encounters, dating from 1932 in modern times. One recent sighting occurred at 4 a.m. on September 18, 2012, reported by a traveler from Fort Scott, Kansas. Soon after crossing the Missouri border on Highway 54, near the town of Nevada in Vernon County, he saw "something" cross the road on two legs. He told the BFRO, "It was covered with thick brown hair and it had to be big because in just two or three steps it was across the road and gone into the forest on the other side." Speaking to investigator Larry Newman, the witness recalled "arms which did not swing forward and back to any great degree," and a "slightly pointed" cone-shaped head.[19]

Around 10 p.m. on October 17, 2014, three bow hunters camped in Johnson's Shut-Ins State Park (Reynolds County) heard "woops and low growls" from the darkness. When the sounds were repeated an hour later, flashlight beams revealed a hairy biped some 7½ feet tall, standing with one arm wrapped around a tree trunk as if "trying to blend in with it." They named the spot "Big Foot Ridge," telling the BFRO, "Every time we hunt there, these Big Foots just will not leave us alone." (BFRO Report #46826)

Mississippi

The Magnolia State, source of twenty-two reports since 1950, produced its latest on January 5, 2006. At 5 p.m., a couple returning from a trip to Alabama on the Natchez Trace Parkway saw a creature race across the road near mile marker 307 in Tishomingo County. It was black and smaller than the other animals so far reported in this chapter, barely five feet tall, if that. It ran "faster than a human, maybe about as fast as a deer can run," but "stumbled slightly at the edge of the road and swung its arms to regain balance then continued across the road and into the tree line." BFRO investigator John Callender interviewed the driver on January 8, learning that the creature's head "didn't look human," being "a little raised in the back" and sloping toward the forehead. Its build was muscular and "very stocky." It ran with arms slightly raised, in the manner of a human jogger.[20]

Bigfoot country, near the Natchez Trace Parkway.
Credit: US National Park Service.

Georgia

The Peach State's modern history includes 114 Bigfoot reports since 1961. At 6:15 a.m. on May 10, 2013, a retired teacher from Alabama was spotting wildlife along Highway 278, near Cedartown, when he saw a tall bipedal figure standing in a grassy field, thirty yards from the road. He estimated its height at eight feet, with tall grass obscuring the creature's lower legs. By the time he stopped his pickup truck, the beast was gone. BFRO investigator Morris Collins found several abandoned mineshafts nearby, and reported the witness being "confident in what he saw."[21]

Wyoming

The Equality State is more equal than some, in terms of Bigfoot sightings, with twenty-eight on file since 1890. Most recently, in May 2007, Native American witnesses living near Riverton, in Fremont County, reported two encounters with a BHM. The first occurred in mid-month, around midnight, as two young women were returning home from a rodeo. The creature walked along US Highway 287, facing directly into their headlights, and left them "very frightened." The second sighting, in broad daylight, happened near a rural home on May 30. BFRO member Brooke Raser deemed the reports "credible and mutually corroborating," but released no further substantive details.[22]

Countryside near Riverton, Wyoming, scene of a May 2007 Bigfoot sighting. Credit: US National Park Service.

Montana

Big Sky Country witnesses have filed forty-three Bigfoot reports since 1978. Around 11:55 p.m. on October 13, 2007, while shuttling railroad workers to their train in Big Horn County, witness "J. G." saw a bipedal figure walking along Decker Highway in front of his van. The pedestrian was "at least eight feet tall," covered in coconut-brown hair eight to ten inches long that looked "almost like it was groomed." He pegged the creature's weight between 600 and 700 pounds. J. G. returned later, searching for tracks or hair snagged on a roadside barbed-wire fence, but found nothing.[23]

 ## West Virginia

The Mountain State logs more Bigfoot reports than most, with eighty-eight on file since 1974. Most recently, at 5:05 p.m. on January 5, 2011, a father and son met the creature while driving through Greenbrier County on Interstate 64, near mile marker 168. The biped ran through heavy traffic, narrowly missed by a truck hauling logs, forcing the driver to slam on his brakes. According to the older witness, it was "covered from the top of his head to the ground with long dark brown hair." While running, "the middle of his shoulder was even with the bottom of the cradle on the log trailer."[24]

 ## Washington

Washington leads the nation in Bigfoot encounters, with 573 reported since 1948. Grays Harbor County is the state's second-most active district, and it produced our most recent sighting on December 26, 2012. Around 2 p.m., five witnesses saw "a very large, hairy, upright form" crossing a residential property on Ocean Shores Boulevard. Remarkably, "it was accompanied by three deer, two in front and one behind...The deer were unconcerned." On January 3, 2013, near the same site, one of the witnesses "smelled something really bad...like a ripe garbage can," and left his home to investigate. Approaching the odor's source, he saw a massive biped rise from the ground to face him directly. "It was hairy and brown," he told the BFRO, "with silver gray hair on its back. It reminded me of a giant pile of steel wool." After a brief face-off, the creature dropped to all fours and "slithered along the ground, going under limbs and up a little rise" until it vanished from sight. Police investigated the sighting and seemed to take it seriously. Speaking later to BFRO member Scott Taylor, the witness described Bigfoot's expression as "friendly and intelligent...He expressed that he feels like he made a friend."[25]

Vermont

Far across the country, Vermont claims five Bigfoot encounters since 1984. The latest comes from Windsor County, where three witnesses met a BHM while "moose spotting" along Tyson Road, outside Ludlow, on October 8, 2005. They saw no moose, but did observe "a large bipedal form cross the road in two strides." Viewed from a range of fifty feet, it was "real big, maybe eight feet tall, [and] hairy." The driver, a hunter of forty years' experience, told the BFRO, "It wasn't anything I had ever seen in the woods." He also recalled hearing "very odd vocalizations" near the same spot, while passing on October 7.[26]

Connecticut

The Nutmeg State has produced eight Bigfoot reports since 1953. At 2 a.m. on February 5, 2009, a restless rural resident went to her kitchen for a glass of milk. While drinking it, she saw a face with "large red glowing eyes" at the kitchen window, prompting her to drop and hide below a counter. When she looked again, the face was gone, and there was nothing visible in her backyard. On other occasions, the witness and her husband report hearing "weird vocalizations" around their home, near Bigelow Hollow State Park. Speaking to BFRO member D. A. Brake, the witness estimated that her Peeping Tom was seven feet tall with eyes the size of golf balls, "set farther apart than human eyes." Its facial skin appeared to be light gray.[27]

Massachusetts

The Bay State boasts a surprising twenty Bigfoot encounters since 1978. At 7:02 p.m. on May 4, 2008, a northbound motorist met his BHM on Route 146 near South Uxbridge, one-half mile from the Rhode Island border. Once again, we hear Bigfoot compared to a man in a ghillie suit—an impression dashed when the driver realized the figure stood at least seven feet tall and was covered with shaggy black hair. The driver's passenger missed it completely, distracted by her iPod.[28]

Rhode Island

Little Rhody lags behind its southern neighbor, with five Bigfoot reports since 1998. At 2 a.m. on April 15, 2010, a driver coming from Connecticut on Route 6 East saw a large, hairy biped cross the pavement through her headlight beams, clearing a roadside guardrail in a single "smooth and fluid" stride. Her children slept through the fleeting encounter.[29]

Utah

Located in the heart of the Great Basin, Utah has produced sixty-eight Bigfoot reports since 1964. At 10 p.m. on December 7, 2008, a motorist driving through Daggett County on Highway 44, near Flaming Gorge, saw his headlights reflected by "some eyeballs about six and one half to seven feet in the air." Braking, he turned around to get a better look and saw what he first mistook for a bear standing erect. That impression dissolved as he took in a tall creature covered in "very long black matted hair," walking slowly and without a trace of fear. The same could not be said for its observer, who fled in panic.[30]

Utah's Flaming Gorge. Credit: US National Park Service.

 Texas

We're told that everything is bigger in Texas, and while the Lone Star roster of Bigfoot sightings trails four other states, it stands at a very respectable 200. One recent sighting comes from Sabine County, near San Augustine, on November 25, 2011. A half-hour short of dusk, while hunting deer, the witness glimpsed a shaggy figure she initially mistook for another hunter in a "ghillie" suit. Peering through her rifle's scope, she froze in "instant heart-stopping bone-chilling fear" at the sight of an apelike creature covered with "long, dark, almost black, muddy-like colored hair. The hair had to be eight inches long; its face looked kind of like a gorilla, that black leathery look, but it had human structure." Standing eight feet tall and "very muscled looking," the

A standard hunter's "ghillie" suit. Credit: Author's collection.

biped "seemed in a hurry to get wherever it was going." It passed into a pine thicket, leaving behind a smell "kind of like wild hogs."[31]

On July 9, 2014, the BFRO received a strange report from Cass County logged by father and son fishermen. A few days earlier, while driving to a fishing spot on Wright Patman Lake, the witnesses had met a hairy biped at a location they refused to disclose, allegedly fearing lawsuits from amateur Bigfoot hunters the beast might injure in future. The creature was dark brown, eight to nine feet tall, nearly four feet wide across the chest, and carried a mangled cottonmouth snake in one hand. As the father told the BFRO: "I am a religious man and have the light of God in my heart and Jesus is my lord. I immediately believed I was looking at a demon. I question that now, after talking to people who seem to know a lot about these things, and reading a lot over it since I saw it. Think me mad if you will, but I slammed the vehicle in park, jumped out and started preaching gospel at the thing." Hearing that, the creature allegedly hurled the dead snake at the preacher, "roaring so loud and deep I could feel its vibration," then fled "with otherworldly speed." (BFRO Report #45818)

Tennessee

The Volunteer State lists ninety-three Bigfoot encounters since 1974, the latest coming from Hamilton County in September 2011. The witnesses, husband and wife, could not recall a specific date when they reported the sighting in January 2012, but they placed it near Sale Creek, a town of 2,845 inhabitants. Rounding a curve on Lee Pike, at 11 p.m., they briefly glimpsed a creature in the road that vanished with a single stride. According to the wife, "It was brownish gray in color and it was wet with rain, looked like a long-hair dog when wet." They saw no other details, but pegged the beast's height around seven feet.[32]

North Dakota

The Peace Garden State ties Vermont with six BHM reports logged since 1962. At 2:30 a.m. on August 27, 2005, two brothers saw a hairy giant standing beside County Road 7 near White Shield, in McLean County. The creature was brown and stood seven to eight feet tall, by their estimate. Racing to a cousin's nearby home, the witnesses persuaded two relatives to go back with them, bringing high-powered spotlights. While scanning the wheat fields, one passenger saw a creature moving on all fours that "looked like a gorilla from the movies." After rushing home to phone authorities, they drove back yet again, noting a "smell of pee and old sweet and slew odor." A game warden arrived in due course and joined in the search until 7 a.m., locating several sets of footprints ranging from four to fifteen inches long and two to seven inches wide. On September 9, six witnesses reported a similar creature crossing a nearby road, on the eastern edge of the Turtle Mountain Indian Reservation.[33]

South Dakota

South Dakota nearly triples its northern neighbor's tally of Bigfoot encounters, with seventeen on file since 1977. At 5 a.m. on November 14, 2006, a trucker passing through Gregory County saw a strange, dark-colored creature crouching beside Highway 44, two miles from the Platte-Winner Bridge on the Missouri River. Rising to face the witness, it was "tall enough to look into the top of the passenger's side window"—eight feet above ground on his Sterling Acterra box truck. He kept the incident a secret until June 2011, then reported his sighting to the BFRO.[34]

Pennsylvania

The Keystone State is rife with Bigfoot sightings: 101 since 1973 by the BFRO's tally; 296 between the 1830s and 1989, according to author Rick Berry.[35] At 8:30 a.m. on March 4, 2012, witness David Childers saw one of the creatures from the fourth-floor window of his mother's apartment in a Bethel Park residence for senior citizens. He was watching wild turkeys and deer cross a nearby field, when they were joined by "a very large, very hairy animal that is unknown to me," walking "like two thirds erect…the best I can say is that it looked like a gorilla." Childers, a retired policeman, was "too stunned" to alert his family before the creature disappeared from view. Interviewed by BFRO member Robert Gorny on May 6, Childers described the beast as "a bit taller than six feet, and approximately 250 to 350 pounds, with a massive upper body build. It was covered in dark brown hair, approximately four to six inches long, but not around the upper face," which was dark tan in color.[36]

Oregon

The Beaver State ranks fifth nationwide in modern Bigfoot sightings, with 234 reported since 1984. At 7:15 a.m. on October 23, 2010, a hunter prowling the woods near Hugo, in Josephine County, saw "a very large animal walking upright in front of me across the trail at about ten yards." While not running, it crossed a clearing fifteen to twenty feet wide in two strides. The witness judged it to be seven feet tall, at least, and guessed its weight at 500 pounds. Reporting to the BFRO a week later, he noted, "I don't know what its face looked like. I was fixated on its body. It was just big and muscular with a big rear end. Its head looked like it was sitting almost directly on it's shoulders." His sketch of the creature is posted on the BFRO's website.[37]

Oklahoma

Sooner State witnesses have logged eighty-eight Bigfoot encounters since 1942. Most recently, at 11:30 a.m. on March 18, 2012, one of the creatures showed itself near the west end of Rich Mountain (Le Flore County), in the Ouachita range. An Arkansas couple was approaching the mountain on Highway 88, passing Talimena Scenic Drive, when the woman saw a biped seven to eight feet tall at roadside, covered in "stringy hair of varying shades of brown." As it walked, she saw its "long arms swinging in the usual 'squatchy' way." Her husband missed the hairy hiker, and the narrow, winding road prevented him from turning back. Asked if it might have been a bear, the woman replied, "If I saw a freaking bear, I would have told you it was a bear. I know the difference, and bears don't walk on two legs and they don't have arms." Speaking to BFRO investigator Carter Buschardt, the witness said the beast's "dominant feature was the hands, large, long and human/ape like."[38]

Ohio

T he country's third most active Bigfoot state, Ohio claims 240 BHM encounters since 1974. Near dusk on August 29, 2011, a Hocking County resident was walking her dogs on Goat Run Honey Fork Road, south of Logan, when she heard a high-pitched whistle, followed by rustling sounds in the forest. Looking around, she saw "a tall hairy creature staring at me. It was very dark and let the branch go that it was holding down with its arm and stepped back into the trees." Questioned by BFRO member Russ Jones, the witness described her visitor as eight to nine feet tall, measured by the branch it had pulled down.[39]

New York

K ing Kong aside, the Empire State is not renowned for large primates, but it has logged 100 Bigfoot reports since 1969. At 6:30 p.m. on June 22, 2009, a young driver traveling through Rhinebeck (Dutchess County) saw a grocery bag lying in the middle of Pilgrim's Progress Road. The bag contained an open box of cereal, "and a log placed in the bag." Steering around the obstacle, he glanced at his rearview mirror in time to see a "big, black thing" rush toward the bag, appearing to walk on all fours. Suspecting a bear, he turned back at the first opportunity and returned to find the bag missing. Some 350 yards farther on, he overtook a seven-foot-tall figure walking on two legs. "It was black," he wrote, "and it looked as if the hair was short. Its back was towards me, and the shoulders were very broad. It looked like it was slouching, and I couldn't really see its arms." As he approached, the creature leaped from the pavement and disappeared into tall grass.[40]

Nevada

B est known for its casinos, quickie divorces and legalized prostitution, the Silver State also claims eight Bigfoot sightings since 1972. The latest comes from three witnesses, including a Reno policeman identified only as "Troy," who met their creature in July 2004 and reported it to the BFRO in December 2007. Troy and friends were climbing Boundary Peak, in the White Mountains of Esmerelda County, and were within a few hundred feet of the summit at 2 p.m., when they saw a hairy figure roughly five feet tall scaling a slope 100 feet away. As described by Troy, "This creature would run on two legs upright until it came up on a large boulder, and then it would crawl over it on all four legs and run for a while on all four legs. After a short distance, it would stand back up on two legs and run until it came up to another obstacle...The head area appeared to have long hair around the face and head. It appeared to be a light brown in color with darker hair around the head and groin area." They lost sight of the beast before anyone thought to retrieve the cameras tucked in their packs. BFRO member Richard Hucklebridge reports that Troy "was a non-believer about the Sasquatch phenomenon before this sighting. He is now a 100%'er."[41]

New Mexico

The Land of Enchantment far outstrips Nevada's Bigfoot sighting tally, with forty-one reports collected since 1976. Most recently, at 12:30 a.m. on July 16, 2011, a family en route to a Navajo reunion in the Chuska Mountains (McKinley County) met a BHM near Narbona Pass, on Indian Service Route 32. A full moon and their headlights framed "a big black figure" standing near a roadside pond, its reflection in the water clearly visible. As they approached, the creature ran on two legs up a hill, and out of sight beyond. "It was a quick smooth run," the driver wrote, "Ninja-like, smooth and stealthy. In less than 5–6 seconds it was in the trees."[42]

New Jersey

Besides its reputation for gangsters, gambling, and cutthroat politics, the Garden State also boasts forty-eight modern Bigfoot reports, dating from 1966. At 3 p.m. on April 15, 2011, three campers left their tents for a hike through Morris County's Mahlon Dickerson Reservation. Ascending a trail, the lead hiker glanced to his right and saw "a tall bulky black figure" moving through the nearby trees. "Its arms were long and swung in large motions as it walked," he later wrote. "The head was dome shaped and very close to the shoulders. In fact, it seemed that it would have had to turn its entire body to look in any direction other than straight ahead." Placing his twelve-year-old son at the spot where the creature had stood, the witness concluded that the BHM was "an easy twelve inches taller and three times bigger around" than his five-foot-six, 155-pound son.[43]

New Hampshire

Modern Granite State tales of Bigfoot date from the 1930s, with nine reports from six counties on file in the twenty-first century. Most recently, during summer of 2008, a witness known only as "Mrs. J."

A hiking trail through New Jersey's Mahlon Dickerson Reservation.
Credit: US National Park Service.

claimed multiple sightings of Bigfoot at her home outside Gilford, near Gunstock Mountain (Belknap County). As described to the BFRO, the nocturnal visits occurred on "no particular date or time." She writes: "This creature is about nine feet in height. Dark deep brownish long hair, and walks upright, similar to a human. I have seen it go one direction, then go past the window in the other direction several minutes later, or it just walks away until the next time I see it, which has been about once a year...I am spooked by it, but it hasn't done anything to any of us, except look in the window at us." Visiting the witness in June 2009, BFRO investigator Christopher Noël found a deer rib hanging from a tree, and "some potential tracks, but none good enough to cast." Members of Mrs. J's family also report sightings and strange howls from the nearby forest.[44]

Nebraska

Nebraska is American's ninth least densely populated state, but its scattered citizens have still logged fourteen Bigfoot encounters since 1957. One resident of Douglas County, near Omaha, reports multiple sightings from the age of ten, with the "most vivid" occurring in April 2002. On that occasion, married with children, she heard her dogs barking and stepped outside to find a shaggy monster "leaping" from tree to tree, then advancing toward her in menacing fashion, sparking "overwhelming" fear. She escaped to the house, but reports "something" hurling its ponderous weight against the brick walls on other occasions. Interviewed by BFRO member Stan Courtney in 2005, the witness described her monster from 2002 as seven feet tall, 350 pounds and "very muscular," covered in brown hair "like that of a long-haired dog." Its face featured a "big brow" with deep-set eyes, atop a "fat, wide neck." Its arms were long and apelike, with large hands.[45]

North Carolina

The Tarheel State has produced eighty-six claims of Bigfoot encounters since 1968. The latest comes from a hunter who met the creature near Castalia, in Nash County, at 8:30 a.m. on December 28, 2012. While stalking deer, he saw a creature standing upright, seven and one half feet tall, covered in dark brown hair with reddish highlights. It departed after several seconds, leaving the witness frozen in shock—and yearning for another encounter. Speaking to BFRO member Kevin Zorc, the witness elaborated, describing the creature as forty inches wide across the shoulders, where its "square-shaped head blended into a thick neck." Its hair was four to six inches long on a "heavily muscled" frame. Its "leisurely" departing steps covered thirty-odd feet in four-foot strides. Under questioning, the witness recalled another incident, wherein a "harvested" deer disappeared before its slayer could reach the carcass.[46]

South Carolina

Palmetto State witnesses have logged fifty-two Bigfoot reports since 1964. Around 12:45 a.m. on July 9, 2005, a party of five traveling on Route 321 near the Georgia border saw "a black, hairy, tall thing" cross the foggy road, appearing so abruptly that the driver nearly struck it with his van. It stood upright, "like a person with a slight bent," and was "muscular but not stocky." As described by the driver, "it was taking its time" until his brakes screeched, then "kind of sped up or skipped, to avoid getting hit." When they turned to look back, the seven-foot creature had vanished.[47]

Wisconsin

The Badger State claims seventy-two Bigfoot reports since the 1970s. At 3 a.m. on July 12, 2013, two fishermen en route to a tournament near Phillips (Price County) saw a "big black animal" on East Wilson Flowage Road standing with its back to their headlights. At their approach, "it ran into the woods [and] we could tell that the creature had a 45-degree angled back from head to rear end. Not at all like a bear. Additionally, it ran into the woods using its front two arms like an ape. Using its knuckles like an ape." BFRO member Bob Barhite questioned witness "Matt" on August 8, clarifying that the creature "didn't use its arms for locomotion; rather it appeared the arms were used only for balance, and its palms were turned outward."[48]

 Michigan

With 180 reports on file since 1965, the Wolverine State appears to be prime BHM territory. At 5:30 p.m. on a Wednesday in April 2012, teenage witness "Michael" was fishing at a pond between Whittemore and Tawas City (Iosco County), when a rock splashed down nearby and he turned to see "this big giant apelike creature" watching him. Before it turned away, growling, he estimated that the biped "stood at least eleven feet in the air." Interviewed later by BFRO investigator Don Peer, Michael allowed that the BHM may have been ten feet tall, but no shorter.[49]

Canada

▶ British Columbia

As an American organization, the BFRO naturally logs most of its cases from the United States, but its files also contain reports from eight of Canada's thirteen provinces and territories. British Columbia leads by a wide margin, with 126 cases dating from 1934. (John Green logged 225 in his last published tally, from 1978.[50]) The latest BFRO sighting comes from Whiteswan Lake Provincial Park, where an elk hunter glimpsed one of the creatures on September 25, 2007. Its appearance was preceded by "a god-awful smell," then the witness saw "something very tall and ugly" standing "stalk straight" among nearby trees. It bolted and vanished before he could grab his rifle. Questioned by BFRO member Blaine McMillan, the hunter described Bigfoot's stench as "almost a cross between a wet dog and a dead animal," which came and went suddenly, as if the beast had "turned it on and off."[51]

▶ Alberta

Next-door, in Alberta, the BFRO has thirty-six Bigfoot reports on file, dating from 1960 (plus a sighting of giant footprints from January 1811). Their most recent "Class A" sighting occurred in April 2005, on Highway 16 north of Stony

Plain, outside Edmonton. Around 10 a.m., a motorist and her teenage daughter saw a light brown creature "the size and shape of a large chimp," walking at roadside "with a two-armed swinging motion." They did not stop, and quickly lost sight of the animal. Questioned by Blaine McMillan in February 2006, the adult witness—a forestry worker—explained that the beast had run on all fours, "with the ends of the front limbs not ending in paws like a bear but on folded hands much like a gorilla or chimpanzee."[52]

► Manitoba

The BFRO's files contain thirty-seven reports from Manitoba, dating from 1941 (when witness "Peter" claims he killed a Sasquatch near Basket Lake, mistaking it for a moose). The latest "Class A" sighting comes from the vicinity of Clearwater Lake Provincial Park, near The Pas, where a child camping with his parents met the creature in May 2007. The boy described a black-haired biped roughly eight feet tall—the height of his living room ceiling at home—with a head "slightly peaked but still rounded." When seen, it was "scraping on a tree with both hands then pounding with one hand raised upward," to produce loud knocking sounds often reported in association with Bigfoot. The boy refused to speak with BFRO investigator Blaine McMillan, but McMillan found the mother's second-hand account "very credible."[53]

Manitoba's Clearwater Lake Provincial Park. Credit: Parks Canada.

▶ Ontario

Canada's most densely-populated province still has plenty of wilderness landscape, and it has contributed sixty-seven Bigfoot reports to BFRO files since 1964. At 9:30 a.m. on August 15, 2008, a couple strolling near their summer cabin, outside Westport, saw "a man" walking through the woods some fifty yards away. A double-take revealed that their visitor was naked and covered in hair, "with different colored brown patches and one patch of hay colored yellow on its side that stood out in the sun." It stood over six feet tall, walking "with a fluid grace and in three long strides crossed the clearing." Later that morning, the couple heard branches snapping in the woods behind their cabin. Two months after the initial sighting, at 1 a.m. on October 11, the witnesses heard strange "oooo" cries and sounds of something rummaging around outside their dwelling, ending when the man turned on an exterior light.[54]

▶ Québec

Moving northeastward, we draw our next Bigfoot sighting from Nunavik, the northern third of Québec, with some 12,000 Inuit tribe members occupying 171,307 square miles north of the 55th parallel. On October 19, 2013, five hunters were stalking caribou on the Hudson Bay coast, south of Akulivik, when they spied an "unexpected something" atop a small hill. It was tall and hairy, and the sighting was preceded by "the sound of something throwing rocks." Though hungry, they declined to shoot the BHM because "it walks like a human, with long, long arms." Their sighting brought to light another case, from September 2012, when a Bigfoot frightened two berry-pickers near Akulivik. On that occasion, the creature left sixteen-inch footprints.[55]

▶ New Brunswick

The largest of Canada's Maritime provinces has reported seven Bigfoot encounters since 1983, according to the BFRO. Around 4:30 p.m. on June 6, 2006, a Michigan couple driving on New Brunswick Route 2 near Sackville saw a figure cross a forest clearing, roughly 100 yards from the highway. Although they "seldom agree on anything," both concurred that it was Bigfoot, dark in color, six to seven feet tall, and walking "in a casual manner." As best they could tell from a distance, "the face appeared all dark."[56]

Thus ends our sampling of the latest cases logged at press time for this book. They are a mere suggestion of the eyewitness accounts on file, but they establish the consistency of most reports, along with deviations in the creatures' size and color that effectively rule out a far-flung web of hoaxers clad in mail-order costumes. Unless we treat the witnesses en masse as lunatics or liars, they have seen something—more specifically, a something that defies mainstream zoology.

And so the hunt begins.

CHAPTER 3

ON THE TRACK

Some Bigfoot hunters devote their lives to the quest, either living on a shoestring budget and spending every spare cent on the search, or finding ways to make their projects pay—through writing, leading guided tours, producing films or television shows, whatever. Others hunt as time allows, on weekends or vacations from their normal jobs that make ends meet. A few have managed both, building careers in fields ranging from academia to entertainment, finding ways to merge the two. This chapter introduces the best-known "Bigfooters," and some who may be more obscure, then examines the methods they use when seeking Bigfoot.

Who's Hunting?

▶ **John Willison Green**, born in February 1927, is the grand old man of Bigfoot hunting, known to some as "Mr. Sasquatch" for the decades he's invested in the search and his massive database of 3,000-plus sightings and footprint reports. A Canadian by birth, residing in Agassiz, British Columbia, Green joined the hunt at age thirty after meeting Swiss-Canadian researcher René Dahinden and has been on the case ever since. His first major investigation was the Bluff Creek flap of 1958, and Green has been relentless in collecting data from all parts of North America. His published books include:

- ▶ *On the Track of the Sasquatch* (1968),
- ▶ *Year of the Sasquatch* (1970),
- ▶ *The Sasquatch File* (1973),
- ▶ *Sasquatch: The Apes Among Us* (1978),
- ▶ *On the Track of the Sasquatch, Book 2* (1980),
- ▶ *Encounters with Bigfoot* (1994), and
- ▶ *The Best of Sasquatch Bigfoot* (2004).
- ▶ A tribute to Green was staged at Harrison Hot Springs on the weekend of April 8–10, 2011, with presentations from other Bigfooters including Dr. John Bindernagel and Dr. Jeffrey Meldrum.[1] Green remains active, as age allows, and you may find his database online at www.sasquatchdatabase.com.

▶ **Loren Coleman** may be America's best-know authority on Bigfoot and other "monsters." Over the past decade, it is a rare TV program on Bigfoot that does not include an interview or commentary from him. Born in Virginia (1947) and raised in Illinois, Coleman presently resides in Portland, Maine, where he owns and operates the International Cryptozoology Museum (dubbed New England's "best quirky museum" by *Yankee* magazine in 2010).[2] Over the years, he has balanced a university teaching career with extensive fieldwork on Bigfoot and other elusive cryptids. His books devoted to Bigfoot, wholly or in part, include:

- ▶ *Creatures of the Outer Edge* (with Jerome Clark, 1978),
- ▶ *Mysterious America* (1983, updated 2007),
- ▶ *Tom Slick and the Search for Yeti* (1989),
- ▶ *Cryptozoology A to Z* (with Clark, 1999),
- ▶ *The Field Guide to Bigfoot, Yeti, and Other Mystery Primates Worldwide* (with Patrick Huyghe, 1999),
- ▶ *Bigfoot! The True Story of Apes in America* (2003),
- ▶ *Monsters of New Jersey* (with Bruce Hallenbeck, 2010),
- ▶ *True Giants: Is Gigantopithecus Still Alive?* (2010, with Mark Hall), and
- ▶ *Monsters of Massachusetts* (2013).
- ▶ His extensive website may be found at http://lorencoleman.com.

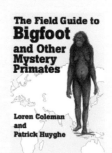

One of Loren Coleman's many books on cryptozoology.
Credit: Author's collection.

▶ **Jerry Dale Coleman** is Loren's brother, born in 1951, and the two are sometimes at odds, with Jerry quick to criticize his elder sibling (often indirectly or anonymously). The oblique sniping is most obvious in Jerry's books, *Strange Highways* (2003) and *More Strange Highways* (2006), and in his Internet blog, including shots at unspecified persons who "call themselves Cryptozoologists"— which is Loren's normal introduction on TV shows and the banner headline on his website—and attacks on specific comments from Loren or articles he's written. A typical broadside reads:

Over analyzing and speculating on cases, even going so far as to assume the sex life of Bigfoot or the unknown origins of Nessie at Loch Ness as well as referring to obscure related bits as puzzle pieces of evidence is as counter productive as an armchair Cryptozoologist can dreadfully hope to become. On the surface it may appear constructive to many but the simple truth of the matter is it's a cheap, inexpensive, non-threatening, lazy way to promote another personal theory, entertain ones self [*sic*] or stir a debate rather than perform or initiate [a] sound productive framework to get to the truth.[3]

Thankfully, the brothers seemed to patch it up, more or less, by 2006, when Jerry wrote, "So even though there still exists a line in the crypto-sand between Loren and I, and no doubt always will, it's one that we can reach across and shake hands."[4] Loren reciprocated in 2011, with a warm birthday tribute to Jerry on his Cryptomundo blog.[5]

▶ **Ken Gerhard** is another prominent and well-regarded cryptozoological researcher, known to millions of Americans for his appearances on television programs including:

▶ *MonsterQuest*,
▶ *Legend Hunters*,
▶ *Paranatural*,
▶ *Monster Project*,
▶ *Ultimate Encounters*,
▶ *The Unexplained Files*,
▶ *The Real Wolfman* (a History Channel special), and
▶ *Weird or What?*

Ken Gerhard, world-renowned Texas cryptozoologist and author. Credit: Ken Gerhard.

▸ Born in October 1967, one week to the day before Roger Patterson filmed his purported Bigfoot in California, Gerhard presently resides in Texas, where he serves as a field representative for the British-based Centre for Fortean Zoology (CFZ) and the Gulf Coast Bigfoot Research Organization (GCBRO). His books (thus far) include:
▸ *Big Bird!* (2007),
▸ *Monsters of Texas* (with Nick Redfern, 2010), and
▸ *Encounters with Flying Humanoids* (2013).
▸ Ken combines home turf research with widespread travel on six continents, plus contributions to the CFZ's *Animals and Men*, *Bigfoot Times*, *Fate Magazine*, and *The Journal of the British Columbia Scientific Cryptozoology Club*. Follow his latest adventures and investigations on Facebook.

▶ **Nicholas "Nick" Redfern** is a native of England, born in 1964, residing since 2001 in Texas, where he works closely with Ken Gerhard. A best-selling author in his own right, Nick launched his journalistic career in 1981 writing for *Zero*, a British magazine covering fashion and rock music, then moved on to freelancing to various prominent newspapers and periodicals from 1996 onward. He broke into Forteana—the study of natural mysteries and the paranormal— with a trilogy of books on Ufology, published worldwide by Simon & Schuster of London between 1997 and 2000. A relentless pursuer of classified government files, Nick has also been featured on TV programs including:

▸ *MonsterQuest*,
▸ *Paranatural*, and
▸ *Proof Positive*.
▸ His books on cryptozoology include:
▸ *Three Men Seeking Monsters* (2004),
▸ *Memoirs of a Monster Hunter* (2007),
▸ *Man-Monkey* (2007),
▸ *There's Something in the Woods* (2010),
▸ *Monsters of Texas* (with Gerhard, 2010),
▸ *Monster Diary* (2012),
▸ *Wildman!* (2012), and
▸ *Monster Files* (2013).
▸ Check out his website at www.nickredfern.com.

Nick Redfern, current Texas resident, field investigator, and best-selling Fortean author. Credit: Nick Redfern.

▶ **Dr. Don Jeffrey Meldrum** is a full professor of anatomy and anthropology at Idaho State University, also serving as an adjunct professor of occupational and physical therapy. Born in 1958, he is a world-renowned expert on foot morphology and locomotion in primates, which led him to the study of Bigfoot through the examination of various footprint casts. Today, despite his many mainstream academic achievements and publications, he remains closely associated in the public mind with Bigfoot—a personal choice that has sparked heated controversy among some of Meldrum's colleagues. After his appearance on the 2003 TV special *Sasquatch: Legend Meets Science*, there were "grumblings" about his tenure at ISU—though no formal requests for review—and Martin Hackworth, a senior lecturer in the physics department, seemed particularly bitter. Calling Meldrum's research "a joke," Hackworth went on to say, "Do I cringe when I see the Discovery Channel and I see Idaho State University, Jeff Meldrum? Yes, I do. He believes he's taken up the cause of people who have been shut out by the scientific community. He's lionized there. He's worshipped. He walks on water. It's embarrassing." Meldrum replies, "Is the theory of exploration dead? I'm not out to proselytize that Bigfoot exists. I place legend under scrutiny and my conclusion is, absolutely, Bigfoot exists."[6] Brian Dunning strove for balance on his Skeptoid blog, aptly noting that:

Dr. Jeffrey Meldrum, with a footprint cast from his extensive personal collection. Credit: Jeff Meldrum

Dr. Meldrum is responsible for drumming up his own grant money from private donors to fund any Bigfoot research that he chooses to do. In some cases, he has received small amounts of matching funds from the university. If you feel this was a bad expenditure, then criticize the university regents who decided to write the check, don't criticize the person they gave the funds to. The work of responsible scientists like Dr. Meldrum is exactly what true skeptics should be asking the Bigfoot community for, not criticizing him for it.[7]

Meldrum's many publications include two on Bigfoot: *Sasquatch: Legend Meets Science* (2006) and *Sasquatch Field Guide* (2013).

▶ **Matt Moneymaker** is best known today for his TV series *Finding Bigfoot*, airing on Animal Planet since 2011 (see Chapter 8). The son of a prominent bankruptcy lawyer, Moneymaker was born in Hollywood, California, in 1965, and developed an interest in Bigfoot at age eleven, after viewing various documentary features. Prior to graduating from UCLA in 1992, he corresponded with other researchers and made his first track discovery in 1987. Moving on to Ohio's University of Akron School of Law, Moneymaker earned his J.D. in 1996, a year after founding the BFRO. Two years prior he reportedly logged a personal sighting of Bigfoot near Kent, Ohio. Upon graduation, he skipped the bar exam in favor of launching the BFRO's website, with a present database of some 28,000 sightings and track reports. Still president of the BFRO, he wrote and co-produced the Discovery Channel documentary *Sasquatch: Legend Meets Science* and the Outdoor Life Network's *Mysterious Encounters* series (2003-04). While not, as some sources claim, the first person to record purported Bigfoot vocalizations, Moneymaker is a pioneer in "call blasting" and an early proponent of linking Bigfoot to "deer kill stashes" in the wild. Ranked seventh on a Facebook list of the Top 100 figures in Bigfoot research, his work is summarized there as follows:

Creator of the Habituation theory [see below]. Although not a favorite in the Bigfoot community he has done great work to legitimize [Bigfoot research]... recording Howls in Ohio that are some of the best. We do think that MM is too much on the side of BF being Ape-like and does not give the Big Guy credit for its intelligence.[8]

▶ **Christopher Noël** holds a Master's degree in Philosophy from Yale University and taught for twenty years at the Vermont College of Fine Arts before devoting himself full-time to Bigfoot studies in 2005. He ranks second on the Top 100 list mentioned above, credited there as author of the "Bigfoot is plentiful theory" and the "backyard Bigfoot theory" (though Lisa Shiel apparently coined the latter phrase in 2008), and also a primary "habituation researcher."[9] His publications in the field include:

- *Impossible Visits* (2009),
- *Sasquatch Rising 2012* (2013), and
- *How Sasquatch Matters* (2014).
- A promotional blurb for his latest work describes it a: the only available source to not only delve into the scientific revolution unfolding before us today but also to fill in the rest of the story, conducting readers behind the scenes at multiple habituation sites—in Iowa, New York State, North Carolina, Oklahoma, Texas, and Vermont. These first-person testimonials and the author's own field notes show the subtle, surprising ways of our ancient living kin."[10]

Noël's views are controversial among Bigfoot researchers and widely scorned by debunkers, but he stands his ground and states his case, leaving the final judgment to his readers.

► **Hawk Spearman** lives in Ashville, Alabama—population 2,212 in 2010—and once led the Southeastern Bigfoot Research Organization from his home. He claims two personal sightings, the first of several hairy bipeds whom, he decided, were not "men in costumes, cause I could see their muscles flex."[11] One lobbed a rock at Spearman, prompting him to flee. The second encounter produced a ten-second videotape of an apparent apelike creature staring at Spearman through trees near his former home in Ohio. While his present focus is the Southeastern United States, Spearman fields calls from across the country. He has apparently stepped down as leader of the SBRO, and its website is no longer found online, though researcher Jason Williams maintained a Facebook page for the group in 2013, still viewable at www.facebook.com/SBRG2011.

► **Dr. John Bindernagel** is a wildlife biologist whose fascination with Bigfoot began as a third-year student at Ontario's University of Guelph. From there, he earned a PhD. in biology from the University of Wisconsin–Madison, then moved to British Columbia, as he writes, "partly in order for myself to begin field work on this species." In 1988, Bindernagel and his wife found several Bigfoot tracks near their home on Vancouver Island, and while plaster casts of those footprints remain his "only tangible evidence...for the existence" of Bigfoot, Bindernagel writes: "Wildlife biologists regularly depend on tracks and other wildlife sign as evidence for the presence of bears, deer, wolves, and other mammals. We recognize that tracks constitute more reliable and persistent evidence of a mammal species than a fleeting glimpse of the animal itself."[12] A longtime curator for the BFRO, Bindernagel has published two books on Bigfoot: *North America's Great Ape: The Sasquatch* (1998) and *The Discovery of the Sasquatch* (2010).

▶ **Autumn Williams** first glimpsed Bigfoot with her mother before her third birthday. A lifelong fascination with the creatures propelled her into research and prominence in the field. She hosted the Outdoor Life Network's *Mysterious Encounters* program in 2003-04. Williams also established (and still maintains, at this writing) the Oregon Bigfoot website—which, despite its title, offers a database of 1,393 Sasquatch encounters nationwide. Battling serious health issues, Williams announced her retirement from active field research in October 2010, five months after publication of *Enoch: A Bigfoot Story*, which depicts ongoing interactions between protagonist "Mike" and the titular Bigfoot. Autobiography or clever fiction? Readers have argued that point since the book's first appearance, with no end to squabbling in sight.

Enoch, the quasi-autobiographical novel of Bigfoot habituation, by Autumn Williams. Credit: Author's collection.

▶ **Cliff Barackman**, a California native now living in Oregon, divides his time between music and Bigfoot research, sometimes spending as much as 200 days per year in the field. From home, he runs the North American Bigfoot blog, where he describes himself (in third person) as "a dedicated Sasquatch field researcher for the past two decades. Known throughout the Sasquatch scientific community for his extended expeditions, he has...managed to gather data supporting the hypothesis that Sasquatches are an undiscovered species of great ape that walks bipedally and lives in North

Cliff Barackman (right), with colleague Craig Flipy, on the cover of his *Bigfoot Road Trip* DVD. Credit: Author's collection.

America."[13] Barackman is the star and producer of *Bigfoot Road Trip*, a DVD chronicling eight expeditions with colleague Craig Flipy.

▶ **Dr. Esteban Sarmiento** received his Ph.D. in 1985 in biological anthropology and spent the next thirteen years as a research associate at the American Museum of Natural History, chiefly studying hominoid skeletons. Like Dr. Jeffrey Meldrum, he was featured in the television special *Sasquatch: Legend Meets Science*, and has appeared on episodes of the *MonsterQuest* series. He stops short of endorsing Bigfoot's existence, and at times appears to play the role of devil's advocate. In 2003, for example, he said of monstrous tracks discovered through the years, "Either the forgers are spending an awful lot of time on this, or there is reason to give this evidence another look. I think a serious scientific inquiry is definitely warranted."[14] Two years later, Sarmiento himself produced fake footprint casts with dermal ridges, indicating that such casts may not be trusted.[15] He joined in a televised analysis of the controversial Skookum body cast (see Chapter 5), and also told attendees at the 2009 Texas Bigfoot Conference, "If the animal in the [Patterson] film is real, this animal is exceedingly human-like. It would be our closest relative on earth."[16]

▶ **Bobby Hamilton**, a former professional wrestler born in 1952, dates his obsession with Bigfoot from age five, when he says one of the creatures peered through a bedroom window of his Texas home, seeming to beckon Hamilton outside. "I think he may have been looking for an easy meal, and thought he could catch a child," Hamilton told the *Houston Press* in 2003. "Or maybe it was a female Bigfoot who had lost a baby and was trying to take a human away to replace it. I had no idea what it was. I thought I had seen the devil." A living nightmare ensued, with similar sightings by two of Hamilton's siblings, a slaughtered calf, screams in the night and pounding on the house, a horse driven mad by fear, finally forcing Hamilton's family to relocate. Nonetheless, by age eight, Hamilton says, "I knew then and there that I was going to devote my life to hunting Bigfoot."[17] Bankrolled by a thriving construction business, Hamilton founded the Gulf Coast Bigfoot Research Organization (GCBRO) in February 1997, driven by a conviction that the American South was fertile soil for fieldwork. Since then, the GCBRO "has exploded with new members, who are either strong believers or have had a Bigfoot encounter of their own, so there is no skepticism amongst any members of our group as far as the existence of these animals is concerned."[18] Despite its name, the GCBRO maintains an online database of Bigfoot encounters from forty-six US states, plus more from Canada, Europe, and Australia.

► **Eric Altman** is a journalist, historian, media critic, and the dean of Pennsylvania paranormal research. Documentaries depicting Bigfoot fired his imagination at age ten, in 1980, and he began active fieldwork in 1997, as a member of the BFRO. A year later, he joined the Pennsylvania Bigfoot Society (PBS), and serves today as its director. Always eclectic in his pursuit of Fortean topics, Altman also hosts and produces "Beyond The Edge Radio" with colleagues Sean Forker and Lon Strickler (Visit www.beyondtheedgeradio.com). Beyond the Bigfoot field, Altman is a tireless researcher and reporter of diverse cryptid encounters, UFO sightings, and sundry paranormal happenings. The PBS website offers an interactive map with Bigfoot sightings collected by county.

► **Christopher L. Murphy** dates his interest in Bigfoot from 1993, a year before he retired from the British Columbia Telephone Company. Son Daniel, enrolled in a college anthropology class, chose to make a presentation on Bigfoot, driven by his father to interview veteran monster hunter René Dahinden. Their conversation led Murphy into marketing posters and footprint casts, and from there to writing about Bigfoot himself. His books include:

  ▸ *Meet the Sasquatch* (with John Green and Thomas Steenburg, 2004),
  ▸ *The Bigfoot Film Controversy* (2005),
  ▸ *Bigfoot Encounters in Ohio* (with Joedy Cook, 2006),
  ▸ *Bigfoot Film Journal* (2008),
  ▸ *Know the Sasquatch/Bigfoot* (2010), and
  ▸ *Sasquatch in British Columbia* (2013).

► **Barton Nunnelly** describes himself as "a simple Kentucky boy" and "just an ordinary fellow who's experienced more than his share of the extraordinary." Those events include a Bigfoot sighting, but he urges others "to keep in mind that Bigfoot is merely one aspect of the larger 'Beastman' puzzle. We have the apemen, sure, but we also have dogmen, lizardmen, frogmen, mothmen, birdmen, batmen…the list is almost endless."[19] While some may question his unusual good fortune when it comes to sighting cryptids, Bart's evident sincerity and commitment to the quest shines through in his published work, including:

  ▸ *Mysterious Kentucky* (2007),
  ▸ *The Inhumanoids* (2011), and
  ▸ *Bigfoot in Kentucky* (2012).
  ▸ He also collaborated in production of the documentary film *Hunt the Dogman* (2007), from Grendel Films. At one time, Bart owned the Kentucky Bigfoot website, but his name was not in evidence among the site's researchers as this volume went to press.[20]

▶ **Dr. Wolf-Henrich ("Henner") Fahrenbach** boasts some of the most impressive credentials claimed by any Bigfoot researcher. Born in Germany in 1932, he earned a Ph.D. in zoology at the University of Washington (1961), followed by a postdoctoral fellowship in the Department of Anatomy at the Harvard Medical School (1961-63), served as the head of the Laboratory of Electron Microscopy at the Oregon Regional Primate Center (1967-97), and served as a clinical affiliate professor in the Department of Integrative Biosciences at the Oregon Health & Sciences University's School of Dentistry (1987-2007). His esteemed academic publications, dating from 1954, include the article "Sasquatch: Size, Scaling and Statistics," published in the peer-reviewed journal *Cryptozoology* (1998). Widely renowned as an expert in identifying hairs, Fahrenbach has collected more than a dozen purported samples from Bigfoot sighting areas, but diagnostic DNA sequencing has been unsuccessful thus far. In 2003, Fahrenbach presented his paper "The Skin and its Appendages" at Willow Creek's International Bigfoot Symposium. In 2009, he taught a course titled "Bigfoot: An Introduction to Sasquatch, North America's Great Ape" for the Lifelong Learners program at the Superstition Mountain Campus of Central Arizona College. Some critics consider his statements on Bigfoot hyperbolic, as when he told a Texas audience in 2008, "They can cover ninety feet in just three steps, or thirty feet per step. Sasquatch has been observed walking with two 200-pound pigs under his arm through the countryside. On another occasion, he's been witnessed grabbing three goats with one arm and walking over a five-foot fence without breaking stride."[21] Nonetheless, those claims have been collected from eyewitnesses, and it seems churlish to attack the messenger.

▶ **Craig Woolheater** dates his interest in cryptids and Fortean phenomena from age nine, inspired by front-page reports of the "Lake Worth Monster" in the *Fort Worth Star-Telegram*. After viewing *The Legend of Boggy Creek*, Woolheater says, "Bigfoot was something I thought about when I was in the out of doors. On Boy Scout campouts, walking through the woods at night and just being in wooded areas, I thought about encountering Bigfoot."[22] His wish came true in May 1994, while driving with his wife near Alexandria, Louisiana. That sighting led to further study in cryptozoology, and to the formation of the Texas Bigfoot Research Center in 1999, presently known as the North American Wood Ape Conservancy, a tax-exempt non-profit scientific research organization. Woolheater's name did not appear on the group's list of directors as this book went to press,[23] but he remains active in the field and writes a blog on the Cryptomundo website. He is featured in the film documentaries *Squatching* (2005) and *Southern Fried Bigfoot* (2007).

▶ **Robert W. Morgan**, a native Ohioan, reported his first Bigfoot sighting in 1957, turned to full-time research on the creatures twelve years later, and founded the American Anthropological Research Foundation in 1974. A navy veteran, Morgan has an associate degree in electronics from Ohio Technical Institute, plus advanced degrees in electronics and data processing from the Federal Aviation Administration Academy. His biography online claims Morgan created the concept for TV's popular *In Search of...* series (1977-82), hosted by Leonard Nimoy, but that could not be verified at press time.[24] In 1996, Morgan produced an audio cassette titled *Bigfoot: The Ultimate Adventure*, which is still available online. In 2008, he published the *Bigfoot Observer's Field Manual*, available in both print and CD versions. Morgan is deemed controversial in some quarters for his views on what he calls the "Forest Giant People,"[25] and in 2007 he became embroiled in the story of "Bugs," an alleged Texas hunter who claimed to have killed two hairy bipeds in the 1970s (see Chapter 4).

A press clipping announces one of Robert Morgan's Bigfoot expeditions.
Credit: Author's collection.

▶ **Thomas Steenburg**, ranked by one source as "the most tenacious and renowned Canadian investigator of the new Millennium,"[26] first heard of Bigfoot at age five or six, pursuing his interest as a casual hobby until age forty-one, when he decided, "If I don't do this now, I probably never will."[27] Settling in British Columbia, he plunged into active field research, collecting data across western Canada. Steenburg's books on Bigfoot include:

▸ *Sasquatch in Alberta* (1990),
▸ *Sasquatch Bigfoot* (1993),
▸ *In Search of Giants* (2000), and
▸ *Meet the Sasquatch* (with John Green and Christopher Murphy, 2004).

▶ **Dave Shealy's** own website describes him as "the Jane Goodall of the Florida Everglades," a tireless researcher who "has spent his entire life studying a smelly hominid cryptid known as the Skunk Ape, and has established the official Skunk Ape Research Headquarters in Ochopee, Florida." Since meeting one of the creatures himself at age ten, Shealy has pursued all available leads and developed techniques of "baiting" his prey with deer liver and lima beans, which he describes as "a Skunk Ape's favorite treat."[28] In July 2000, Shealy aired video footage of a supposed Bigfoot creature trudging through swampy terrain. Viewable online, the tape still inspires heated controversy today. Shealy has authored the *Everglades Skunk Ape Research Field Guide*, available at his gift shop and for online purchase.

▶ **Michael Johnson** is the driving force behind Sasquatch Investigations of the Rockies, founded in 2009 with longtime friend Scott Barta. Johnson dates his first discovery of a seventeen-inch footprint from the mid-1990s, and claims a personal Bigfoot sighting from the Pikes Peak area near the end of that decade. Other members of the Colorado team include Ron Peterson, David Ottke, Jeff and Theresa Yelek, Jon and Robin Roberts, Tony Lombardo, and Kristi DeLoach (who, in 2012, discovered "a small valley where she and her family have spent many hours interacting with the Sasquatch)."[29]

▶ **John and Montra Freitas** are former BFRO researchers who married and followed a diverging path in Bigfoot research. John was a pioneer of "call blasting," and he takes pride in debunking hoaxes such as the 2005 Sonoma footage hoaxed by comics Penn and Teller, which deceived the BFRO (see Chapter 6). Montra claims a close-up Bigfoot sighting near Sonora, California, in 1978 and later joined Bob and Kathy Strain to stage the first two Bigfoot training camps—"Operation Odyssey" and "Operation Odyssey II"—in 2004 and 2007. In 2001, Montra and her brother investigated Bigfoot sightings near California's Marble Mountain, obtaining video footage of a creature presumed responsible for erecting a crude "hut" or "nest."[30] In addition to call blasting, John, Montra, and their BlueNorth team use bait and pheromone chips in an effort to lure Bigfoot within camera range.

▶ **Bob and Kathy Strain** are married researchers operating from Northern California, where both hold leadership positions in the Alliance of Independent Bigfoot Researchers (AIBR). At press time for *Seeking Bigfoot*, Kathy served as vice-chair under founder Tom Yamarone, while Bob was one of five directors. Bob glimpsed Bigfoot through a rifle's scope in 1975 while hunting in Idaho's Salmon Wilderness and was hooked for life. The couple met at a Bigfoot conference, Kathy already fascinated by aboriginal legends of cannibal giants and films such as *The Legend of Boggy Creek*. Kathy, employed after college as an anthropologist for the Stanislaus National Forest, found time to pursue her passion in territory known for numerous Bigfoot encounters. She is the author of *Giants, Cannibals & Monsters: Bigfoot in Native Culture* (2008). She has also appeared on multiple episodes of TV's *MonsterQuest*.

▶ **Tom Yamarone**, founder of the AIBR, is a California singer/songwriter whose fascination with BHMs developed from attending Willow Creek's 2003 International Bigfoot Symposium. He joined the BFRO in May 2004, scouring mountains and forests for hard evidence. On the side, Yamarone also composed sundry songs for the creature, performing them at venues including the 2005 Sasquatch Research Conference in Bellingham Washington; the 2006 Bigfoot Rendezvous in Pocatello, Idaho; and the 2012 Bigfoot Discovery Day in Santa Cruz, California. As if all that were not enough, he also is a sponsor of and volunteer at the Bigfoot Discovery Museum in Felton, California.

⟲ BIGFOOT TIMES

10926 Milano Avenue, Norwalk, California 90650-1638
www.bigfoottimes.net

December 2011

Bigfooters Of The Year

For those who have followed my documentation and writing on the P-G filmsite, you may recall the *Bigfoot Times* from October 2001, in which I described the "big tree," with a picture of the base of the tree on the second page. It had the look and feel of the big tree but it seemed a bit high off the existing sandbar, but I reasoned that over that time span - almost thirty-four years - that much of that forest floor must have been washed away. Also, it was logical in my mind that over the ensuing decades many of the trees seen in the famous Patterson-Gimlin film were either felled by loggers or toppled by the elements, and the late Rene' Dahinden had already noted tree falls in the 1970s.

That "big tree," (shown below) clearly seen in frame #352 of the P-G film that I located in 2001 turned out to be an imposter; too far to the west to be the real deal. I was just plain wrong in that early analysis.

In September 2003 a distinguished field of Bigfooters, John Green, Dr. Jeff Meldrum, Chris Murphy, myself and others descended upon the P-G filmsite, yet no one could clearly tell with certainty the exact whereabouts of the filmsite with physical reference points to seal the deal. John Green was not as studied as the late Dahinden on the filmsite, but Rene' was no longer available to question. At the time I was only able to show the crowds the street but not an exact address, such as 10926 Milano Avenue. Then and later it was my thinking that much of the original P-G filmsite was washed away by the heavy storms this region experiences and that looking for it would be an exercise in futility.

Yet on that sunny September 14th in 2003 in Bluff Creek the P-G film

Above: bookstore owner Steven M. Streufert at the base of the real "big tree," and California State Park Ranger Robert Leiterman, right, near the filmsite. Below: the "big tree," (a Douglas fir) as it looks today, and as it looked in a black and white photo snapped by Peter Byrne in 1972. Photographs courtesy and copyright of Steven Streufert, Rowdy Kelley and Peter Byrne.

1

site stood silent in all her glory and the scholars at hand could not separate the trees from the forest, so to speak.

Unlike another famous site like Dealey Plaza, the P-G filmsite changed its physical appearance to the point of being almost unrecognizable. Yet it was still there, grown up with new growth filling in the clearings where a silent movie star, Patty, walked away from Roger Patterson's Kodak K-100 movie camera in October 1967.

As the years went on the filmsite was photo documented by the likes of Rene' Dahinden; George Haas; John Green and Peter Byrne but in recent years new forest growth camouflaged the existing site to the point of being unrecognizable.

As that happened the Bigfoot community had a field day, conjuring up

Bigfoot Times, the journal written and published by Daniel Perez. Credit: Author's collection.

▶ **Daniel Perez** publishes *Bigfoot Times*, the only newsletter devoted to Sasquatch still active since the demise of Ray Crowe's *Track Record*. Like many other researchers before him, Perez was energized at age ten by *The Legend of Boggy Creek*, propelled by his first viewing of the film into reading and collecting books on BHMs. At fourteen, he began corresponding with veteran researchers John Green and René Dahinden. When not working as a full-time electrician, Perez has traveled widely in search of Bigfoot, including a trip to Russia. He launched *Bigfoot Times*, official organ of his Center for Bigfoot Studies, in 1999. So far, his research has paid off with publication of:

- ▸ *The Bigfoot Directory* (1986),
- ▸ *Big Footnotes* (1988),
- ▸ *Bigfoot at Bluff Creek* (1994), and
- ▸ *Bigfoot: Encounters Past To Present* (with George Eberhart and Steven DeMarco, 2012).

▶ **Diane Stocking** is the founder, president, and treasurer of Stocking Hominid Research, Inc. A Florida native now living in Oregon, she grew up with Skunk Ape reports and later obtained a degree in forestry.

▶ **SHRI vice president Ron Schaffner**, a retired Ohio computer technician, fueled his fascination with cryptozoology on 1960s B-movies and magazine stories,threw it into overdrive by reading John Keel's *Strange Creatures from Time and Space* at age fourteen in 1975. He investigated his first Buckeye Bigfoot report two years later, and by 1980 was self-publishing a *Creature Chronicles* newsletter, filled with cryptid sightings from across the country. In 1995, he was a cofounder of the BFRO, using his own research to supplement the group's archives. Some issues of *Creature Chronicles* may still be found online.

▶ **Donald Young**, a Wisconsin hunting guide and BFRO investigator, reported a personal sighting of Bigfoot on July 12, 2008. On his fourth night camped in Pike County, Young heard a heavy object fall near his tent, as if thrown, and scanned the woods with a thermal imaging camera, catching what he believes to be two BHMs—an adult and a juvenile—hiding nearby. While impressed, Matt Moneymaker acknowledged that the fleeting glimpse of something warm "will not stand on its own to convince the world."[31] Young subsequently filmed another fleeting thermal image near the same location, depicting some small creature climbing a tree, regarded by some as a "baby" Bigfoot.

▶ **Tim Stover** of Ohio met Bigfoot in October 1992, while deer hunting at Salt Fork State Park, near Cambridge, and has devoted himself to the quest ever since. The creature he saw appeared to stand more than seven feet tall and was "a whitish, silvery-gray color, and as weird as it sounds, my first thought was it looked like a hairy old naked man of the woods."[32] Born in 1967, Stover concentrates on searching near his Portage County home, spending thirty to forty hours a week in the woods and employing high-tech camera equipment purchased at a cost of $8,000. In November 2011, he found and cast a seventeen-inch footprint at West Branch State Park in Ravenna, Ohio. Stover has appeared on TV's *Finding Bigfoot*, co-hosts the *Ohio Bigfoot Hunters Radio Show* online with Karlie White, and posts many video clips on YouTube at www.youtube.com/user/tcsjrbigfoot.

▶ **Brian Brown**, a Minnesota native born in 1967, founded *Squatchopedia* online in 2008 (now defunct) and created The Bigfoot Forums, presently self-described as "the Web's most popular one-stop shop for Sasquatch talk."[33] Brown also hosts and produces the *Bigfoot Information Project* podcast and *The Bigfoot Show Blog* (co-hosted with Scott Herriot and Paul Vella). Brown is a former director of the Alliance of Independent Bigfoot Researchers and served as master of ceremonies for the 2008 Annual Bigfoot Conference in Jefferson, Texas.

▶ **Henry J. Franzoni III** of Wyoming serves as tribal data steward for the Columbia River Inter-Tribal Fish Commission, working with the state's four treaty tribes. Researcher Thom Powell (see below) describes Franzoni as "the walking encyclopedia of the Bigfoot phenomenon" and credits him with providing definitive scientific answers to some of the field's most vexing questions, including the troublesome topic of "disappearing" BHMs.[34] That said, Franzoni himself shuns the "Bigfoot" label, preferring traditional names coined by aboriginal peoples, and freely admits that he spent "a decade of avoiding any contact with mainstream Bigfoot Researchers, who I don't get along with very well."[35] His revelations are contained in a self-published volume titled *In the Spirit of Seatco* (2009), no longer available in print but sold online in PDF format. A sample may be viewed at www.henryfranzoni.com/In%20the%20Spirit%20of%20Seatco%201-37.pdf.

▶ **Steve Kulls**, a private investigator with eighteen year's experience, developed a fascination with Bigfoot in childhood and began pursuing active research in 1998. Initially skeptical, he claims three personal sightings and several more "most likely close encounters" over the past decade.[36] Kulls specializes in debunking Bigfoot hoaxes (see Chapter 6) and operates the SquatchDetective website as "a 'no-nonsense' inquiry into the Sasquatch mystery."[37] His published books in the field include *50 Large* (2011) and *What Would Bigfoot Do?* (2012).

▶ **Thom Powell**, a longtime eighth-grade science teacher at Robert Gray Middle School in Portland, Oregon, began closing his lessons in the 1990s with purported footage of Bigfoot—which, at the time, he dismissed out of hand. As he told the *Portland Tribune*, "I used to teach it for years just as a misapplication of science. In other words, it was something that wasn't valid science. It was fanciful; it was baloney. But it was interesting to the kids." A move to rural Clackamas County changed his mind, influenced by conversations with local witnesses and personal field research, including use of motion-activated cameras. "We never got great video," Powell admits, "but we did get some really interesting things. Once I was satisfied that I wasn't being hoaxed, that something genuine was going on, then it gradually began to emerge that the problem was most likely that we're dealing with something that's so intelligent that it knows what you're doing....You're being watched when you're putting out the cameras...they're very sentient beings that are aware of your coming and going."[38] Powell's Bigfoot books include *The Locals* (nonfiction, 2003) and *Shady Neighbors* (a novel, 2011).

▶ **Rhettman A. Mullis Jr.** of Washington State claims two personal Bigfoot sightings, the first at age ten in summer 1977, when he saw a BHM swimming in Puget Sound. A decade later, Mullis founded Sasquatch Investigations and Research and began conducting field research. His second sighting, in 1997, caught a hairy biped bathing in a quarry pond near Marysville. He has also experienced multiple vocalizations, while documenting tracks and purported Bigfoot scat. When not pursuing his "day job" as a college teacher and children's therapist, or working toward completion of his Ph.D. in psychology, Mullis edits and contributes to the Bigfootology website.

▶ **Jaime Avalos**, a former US Marine and registered nurse by trade, tracks BHMs in California's Sierra Nevada mountain range, where he claims to have found footprints of one Bigfoot—identified by shape and dermal ridges—at two locations 500 miles apart. Avalos also experienced a personal sighting in June 2006, while fly fishing in the high country. He networks with other researchers, has worked with Dr. Jeffrey Meldrum on footprint castings, posts many video clips to the "Sierra Sasquatch" YouTube channel, and has been featured on *MonsterQuest*.

▶ **David Paulides** founded North America Bigfoot Search in 2004 (as he writes) "to develop scientific proof that bigfoot/sasquatch does exist."[39] Paulides serves as the group's executive director, while team members include Dr. Robert Alley in Alaska, forensic artist Harvey Pratt in Oklahoma, Richard Hucklebridge in California, and Scott Carpenter in Tennessee. His published books on BHMs include *The Hoopa Project* (2008) and *Tribal Bigfoot* (2009). Paulides has sparked controversy with his defense of hoaxer Ray Wallace and posting excerpts from Wallace's extensive correspondence online. Paulides dubs Wallace "a very intelligent man," adding that "Once you read some of the letters you can tell that Mr. Wallace obtained some information about bigfoot that was absolutely accurate and not widely known in the 1950s–1980s."[40]

▶ **Dr. J. Robert Alley** is a retired professor of anatomy and physiology who holds degrees in anthropology, physical therapy and chiropractic. Active in Bigfoot research since 1974, Alley met the field's leading figures—including René Dahinden and Dr. Grover Krantz—while traveling through Canada and the United States as a rehabilitative health care provider. He is the author of *Raincoast Sasquatch* (2003) and reportedly has a second book in progress titled *Wild Men of the North*.

The Habituators

Readers of this book will be familiar with the work of primatologists such as Jane Goodall and Dian Fossey, who compiled vast knowledge by living in close proximity to chimpanzees and gorillas, respectively. In Bigfoot research, witnesses who claim long-running interactions with BHMs, either individually or in family units, are known as "habituators." Their reports, typically unsupported by substantive physical evidence—and their refusal to attempt collection of such evidence, for fear of unsettling their shaggy visitors—

leaves them subject to ridicule from skeptics, and even from some die-hard Bigfoot believers.

David Paulides of the NABS defines habituation as "a general accommodation to unchanging environmental conditions, making or becoming suitable, adjusting to circumstance." He goes on to say, "The habituation process and how it relates to a Bigfoot, Sasquatch, and hairy man is not a quick endeavor. This process could take years and maybe decades. Slight changes to the physical environment or changes to residents living in the area could alert the biped to unusual and unfamiliar conditions that could trigger an avoidance response." Nonetheless, he writes, cryptically, "There is a habituation occurring in Middle America with the assistance of a wealthy Canadian. He purchased the property and placed a female biologist on the project. This has purportedly been a successful endeavor and photos, video and behavior have been successfully documented. A documentary film is in the works. We have not been involved in this project and have not spoken to any of the involved parties."[41]

THE CREATURE

Personal Experiences with Bigfoot

BY JAN KLEMENT

The Creature (1976), by mystery author "Jan Klement," was the first supposed nonfiction tale of Bigfoot habituation.
Credit: Author's collection.

While we await that film's release, it may he helpful to review the habituation literature presently available. First to appear in print was *The Creature: Personal Experiences with Bigfoot* (1976, reissued in 2009), penned by pseudonymous author "Jan Klement," purporting to describe the author's interactions with a BHM nicknamed "Kong" somewhere in Pennsylvania. Klement's observations of Kong's diet and behavior—including sex with cows—ends with the creature's death and burial at some undisclosed location. An editor's note to the 2009 edition claims that Allegheny Press editor John Tomikel purchased all rights to the story from Klement in 1975, and that Klement was deceased before republication of the work. Loren Coleman speculates that Tomikel— holder of a Ph.D. from the University of Pittsburgh, a long-time university professor and founder of the Pennsylvania Earth Science Teachers Society, author of twenty-four books under his own name—was in fact "Klement." Tomikel, born in 1928, has yet to comment on the matter.

In 2002, Mary Green published *50 Years with Bigfoot*, coauthored with habituator Janice Carter Coy. Long out of print, the book describes Coy's supposed half-century of interaction with BHMs in Monroe County, Tennessee. The tale begins when Carter's father rescues a baby Bigfoot, dubbed "Fox," that he finds trapped beneath a fallen tree, including observations on the creature's diet, "language," sex life, and an incident where Fox knocked Janice from a horse, breaking her leg. By December 2007, personal quarrels dissolved Green's friendship with Carter, but she continues to vouch for the overall veracity of Carter's claims.[42]

Next on the list is Sali Sheppard-Wolford, whose book *Valley of the Skookum: Four Years of Encounters With Bigfoot* (2006) recounts experiences shared with her daughter, future researcher Autumn Williams, around their home at Orting, Washington. Aside from friendly visits by BHMs, the story also includes a Native American spirit guide called "Dream Walker," mysterious lights in the forest, and reports of a 1959 UFO crash near Orting, masked by a subsequent cover-up. Autumn Williams continued her mother's tale, after a fashion, in *Enoch* (2010, discussed above), while leaving readers to conclude whether the story was fact or fiction.

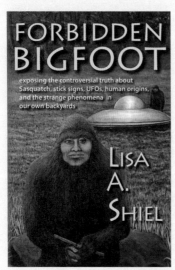

One of several books by author Lisa Shiel, advancing controversial theories about Bigfoot's origins and nature. Credit: Author's collection.

In *Backyard Bigfoot: The True Story of Stick Signs, UFOs, & the Sasquatch* (2006), Lisa Shiel sets out to prove that "Bigfoot and its kin all over the world stand closer to us than we ever imagined."[43] Reviewer Thom Powell praises the book as "a skillfully written combination of field observations, academic perspectives, and discussions of other paranormal mysteries that may relate to the hairy hominid (Bigfoot) mystery. Lisa is daring in her approach: she articulates uncertain evidence, then develops a theory that unifies anthropological mysteries, the Bigfoot phenomenon, and a few other paranormal matters."[44]

A previously mentioned book by Christopher Noël, *Impossible Visits*, tells us "that throughout North America, certain people have been patiently and privately building a much more nuanced, long-term understanding...to learn from this evasive, shrewd and tricky hominid race." It tells "the groundbreaking work of ordinary (and unsung) human beings who have experienced and fostered, sometimes for decades, consistent Sasquatch visitations to their homes and properties. This species has survived alongside Homo sapiens, down through the eons, thanks to enormous stealth, maintaining a necessary margin of physical distance. The 'habituators' have succeeded, not in bridging this distance, but in establishing a rapport that allows for the regular exchange of food and gifts, and even occasional clear daylight sightings."[45]

Another 2011 publication, Julie Scott's *Visits from the Forest People*, details her family's sightings of, and interactions with, BHMs in northeastern Washington

State. While accepting Bigfoot's existence as a flesh-and-blood creature, she speculates that some members of the species can pass between dimensions, while others display an uncanny ability to avoid being photographed.

Predictably, critics heap scorn on such stories. Blogger Robert Lindsay is a typical example, punctuating his reviews with "LOL!" and comments such as "you can see where this shit is heading." He finds it significant that habituators are "often women," and brands Janice Coy specifically as "apparently mentally ill. She has schizophrenia."[46] (That long-distance diagnosis, pronounced without meeting Coy, is apparently lifted from Internet chatter by posters devoid of psychiatric credentials.[47]) While Lindsay's scathing attack sometimes verges on humor, he closes on a jarring note: "I think there have been habituators in past. The Albert Ostman tale from 1924 is credible [more on that later]. American Indians from many tribes say that Bigfoot used to steal their women. Sometimes the women came back after living years with the Bigfoots. In some cases, the women even bred with the Bigfoots. I regard all these stories as credible, but more on that later."[48] Three years on, his readers are still waiting.

Tools and Methods

While most Bigfoot reports are logged coincidentally—by travelers, hikers, and hunters who don't expect to meet monsters—a small community of devotees spend precious time and hard-earned money searching for the Great Unknown. For them, seeking Bigfoot is more than simply a matter of pitching camp in the woods and hoping a BHM may wander by.

Jerry Coleman offers four basic steps toward becoming a hunter for any cryptids. Those steps include:

1. **Commitment and devotion, not necessarily to a "belief" in a certain creature's existence, which may be misguided, but to rigorous investigation and collecting evidence.**
2. **Self-education on the chosen subject, including in-depth study of the extant literature on a given beast, the area(s) where it is said to dwell, and any other necessary subjects: photography, footprint casting, wilderness survival, even local laws concerning planned activities.**
3. **Achieve the proper mindset and maintain it, leaving ego at home, pursuing facts and evidence without commitment to any pet theory.**
4. **If possible, engage in field research. Archivists make a valuable contribution to cryptozoology, sometimes unearthing long-forgotten reports or finding "new" species in dusty museums, but great breakthroughs are made by searchers in the field.[49]**

Once in the field, Coleman has four more simple rules:

1. Document everything, from time of day and weather, to precise locations and minute details about witnesses interviewed.
2. Examine everything at a purported sighting area with notes, photos, and measurements (if relevant).
3. Support eyewitness accounts with copies of official reports (if filed), background research into similar sightings, interviews with neighbors, and thorough examination of any purported evidence collected by witnesses.
4. Record all witness testimony to backstop your memory, avoid later disputes, and to track discrepancies in stories that change over time.[50]

What should you take along while seeking Bigfoot? The obvious answer is, it depends on where you're going, how you're searching, and how long you'll be in the field. Bunking at motels and making day trips into nearby woods will not require the same equipment as protracted camping in the wilderness. If you're not an experienced camper, take time to follow Jerry Coleman's advice by educating yourself on the search area, its terrain, weather patterns, dangerous flora and fauna, and laws pertaining to camping, hiking, and hunting. Every state and major park has guidebooks in print, readily available from libraries, bookstores, or online.

As far as camping goes, if you're a novice, read up on the subject. Some useful sources include:

▸ Michael Hodgson's *Camping for Dummies*,
▸ Paul Tawrell's *Camping & Wilderness Survival*,
▸ Adam Wellman's *Camping Essentials*,
▸ G. A. Iron Cloud's *The Ultimate Camping Guide and Camping Tips*, and
▸ the *SAS Survival Handbook*.
▸ Choice of equipment will depend, at least in part, upon the season and your target area.

Aside from basic camping gear, you'll need equipment chosen with the hunt in mind. A basic list of monster-hunting gear includes:

1. Cameras, with ample film or tape (unless you're shooting digital) and plenty of spare batteries.
2. Communications gear, for contact between hunters and reaching the outside world, in the event of an emergency.
3. Night-vision gear, if you can afford it, for searching after sundown. A quick search online as I wrote this chapter found various devices ranging in price from $99 to $5,000 and up. Again, remember extra batteries.
4. Audio recording equipment, for capturing vocalizations, wood-knocks, and any other "earwitness"-type evidence.
5. Footprint casting materials, in case you get lucky. Any tracks found should be photographed before casting, with photos including a tape measure or other objects to establish scale. Practice casting before you hit the field, to preclude fumbling on the Big Day.

6. **Monster bait, to lure your prey out of hiding.** Diet-wise, BHMs seem to be omnivorous. Witnesses describe them eating everything from nuts and berries to rodents and roadkill, fish caught by hand and clams dug from beaches, fruit from orchards and grub snatched from porches. Other reports add deer, livestock, and humans to the menu. Some BHM hunters recommend pheromone chips, but offer no leads as to where you might find these species-specific items. If you plan on call-blasting, remember to take amplifiers.

A typical camouflaged trail camera, attachable to trees or other stationary objects Credit: Author's collection.

Photographs and tapes of unknown creatures spotted in the wild have marginal value in this age of Photoshop and other techno-wonders. Add in blanket rejections from professional "skeptics," and you may wonder, "Why bother carrying a camera at all?" The simple answer, aside from documenting tracks and other trace evidence, is that you may capture something on film or a memory card that no one else has seen or reported.

Hand-held cameras, including thermographic (infrared) gear, are standard equipment for Bigfoot hunters. Many also use stationary, motion-activated game cameras to mount surveillance on a given site, where bait is present or wildlife signs are plentiful. A search online for *Seeking Bigfoot* found trail cams readily available, ranging in price from $60 to $330; one vendor offered a set of four for $230.

More exotic photo techniques include the "floatograph," employed on TV's *MonsterQuest* and *Mysterious Encounters* series (see Chapter 8), with thermal imaging cameras attached to balloons sent aloft over rugged territory. Jack Osborne has employed a similar technique on his *Haunted Highways* series, using remote-control model aircraft instead of balloons controlled by the wind. In 2012, Dr. Jeff Meldrum proposed "Operation Falcon," using a remote-controlled blimp to search for evidence of Bigfoot, but the estimated $300,000 price tag has proved prohibitive.[51]

Entering the field of Bigfoot research may be as simple as pitching a tent in the wild and hiking alone, but you may also wish to join an active group and play a role in larger, more organized expeditions. Chapter 7 provides contact information for every identified BHM-hunting group active in the US and Canada at press time, plus several in foreign countries. Some are closed groups, while others welcome new members. You may also meet other researchers at regional seminars and conferences. Don Keating's Ohio Bigfoot Conference celebrated

T-shirts advertise the 2014 Ohio Bigfoot Conference.
Credit: Author's collection.

Dr. Jeffrey Meldrum's *Sasquatch Field Guide,* suitable for backpacking. Credit: Author's collection.

its twenty-sixth annual gathering in April 2014. Others are staged nationwide as time and funding permit, advertised online at sites including The Bigfoot Forums.[52] Further contacts are available through social media, such as Facebook. Before paying membership fees to any group, do your homework and determine (a) if the "group" exists in fact, (b) if it performs active research or simply holds discussions online, and (c) what you'll get for your money in terms of publications, access to meetings, and so on.

Whether hunting solo or joining a group, you may profit from reading one or more Bigfoot-specific guidebooks and field manuals. The list includes:

- Peter Byrne's *Monster Trilogy Guidebook*,
- Joedy Cook's *Beginner's Guide to Bigfoot Research*,
- Glenn Edwards's *Squatching*,
- John Hart's *Hiking the Bigfoot Country*,
- Dr. Jeff Meldrum's *Sasquatch Field Guide*,
- Robert Morgan's *Bigfoot Observer's Field Manual*, and
- Dean Russell's *Bigfoot Hunting Project Guide*.

Whether you find a BHM or not, the quest can be invigorating, educational, perhaps opening new frontiers in what has been a humdrum life. If you are reasonably fit and have a modicum of common sense, adventure lies in store!

CHAPTER 4

WANTED: DEAD OR ALIVE?

To be, or not to be? Where Bigfoot hunters are concerned, Shakespeare's classic question gets a twist that leaves some searchers furious: To kill, or not to kill?

In July 2013, Internet blurbs announced the latest television "reality" series focused on Bigfoot, set to premiere on January 10, 2014. As summarized by the show's producers:

Spike TV is raising the stakes in the endless quest to discover the truth about the legendary creature known as Bigfoot, the seemingly mythical being that roams forests of the world, avoiding mankind. The network is announcing a new one-hour reality show, *10 Million Dollar Bigfoot Bounty*, featuring ambitious teams of explorers on a brazen exhibition to unearth real evidence of Bigfoot's existence. The $10 million in cash, underwritten by Lloyd's of London, would be the largest cash prize in television history.[1]

Hosted by former TV Superman Dean Cain, legitimized after a fashion by resident experts Todd Disotell (chief of New York University's Molecular Anthropology Laboratory) and Natalia Reagan (described on her website as "an anthropologist, writer, actress, and comedienne"[2]), the show followed eight teams of hunters, eliminating one each week, until the finalists plunged into "36 Hours of Hell" for an all-out push to the finish line. No one was especially surprised when Bigfoot eluded capture. While the teams focused on digging up forensic evidence, skeptics remained behind their barricades, insisting that the only valid proof of Bigfoot's existence is a more-or-less complete specimen, alive or dead.

Pro-Kill/ No-Kill

On its face, the pro-kill argument seems nearly unassailable. In order to officially identify a species, both the International Code of Zoological Nomenclature and the International Code of Nomenclature for algae, fungi, and plants demand at least one "type specimen" stored in a museum or herbarium research collection, available for study by certified experts. Photographic images have been substituted for type specimens in some cases, but given the state of modern technology they are routinely rejected as proof of Bigfoot's existence.

Faked photo of a supposed dead Bigfoot, created by an anonymous hoaxer. Credit: Author's collection.

As Marcello Truzzi wrote in 1978, "An extraordinary claim requires extraordinary proof."[3]

With that in mind, pro-kill Bigfoot hunters declare that the only way to save Bigfoot is first to bag a specimen, thus opening the way to legal protection of the species—or, in the view of some authors, proving that BHMs are something close to human. While not averse to live captures per se, the pro-kill side has weathered enough disappointments to view the bring-'em-back-alive approach as fruitless.

The list of pro-kill advocates includes late researchers René Dahinden and Dr. Grover Krantz, Canadian John Green, GCBRO founder Bobby Hamilton, and the directors of the North American Wood Ape Conservancy. Ranged against them stand author Loren Coleman, Dr. Jeff Meldrum, leaders of the Mid-America Bigfoot Research Center and the British Columbia Scientific Cryptozoology Club—even People for the Ethical Treatment of Animals.[4] The no-kill group maintains that modern DNA technology can prove existence of a species beyond reasonable doubt, with no requirement for a pickled, mummified, or flayed type specimen in hand.

While the US government ignores Bigfoot, officials in Washington State have taken legal steps to protect BHMs. Skamania County was first, on April 1, 1969, with Ordinance No. 69-01, which reads:

Be it hereby ordained by the Board of County Commissioners of Skamania County:

Whereas, there is evidence to indicate the possible existence in Skamania County of a nocturnal primate mammal variously described as an ape-like creature or a sub-species of Homo Sapiens; and

Whereas, both legend and purported recent sightings and spoor support this possibility, and

Whereas, this creature is generally and commonly known as a "Sasquatch," "Yeti," "Bigfoot," or "Giant Hairy ape," and has resulted in an influx of scientific investigators as well as casual hunters, many armed with lethal weapons, and

Whereas, the absence of specific laws covering the taking of specimens encourages laxity in the use of firearms and other deadly devices and poses a clear and present threat to the safety and well-being of persons living or traveling within the boundaries of Skamania County as well as to the creatures themselves,

Therefore be it resolved that any premeditated, willful and wanton slaying of such creature shall be deemed a felony punishable by a fine not to exceed Ten Thousand Dollars ($10,000) and/or imprisonment in the county jail for a period not to exceed Five (5) years.

Be it further resolved that the situation existing constitutes an emergency and as such this ordinance is effective immediately.[5]

While some note the date and dismiss the law as an elaborate April Fool's joke, commissioners amended it in 1984, barring Bigfoot killers from asserting an insanity defense at trial and permitting prosecution for homicide "should the Skamania County Coroner determine any victim/creature to have been humanoid."[6]

Whatcom County's commissioners unanimously passed Resolution No. 92-043 on June 9, 1992, declaring the entire county a Sasquatch protection and refuge area. All citizens were "asked to recognize said status," although resolutions (unlike ordinances) have no legally binding effect.[7]

Texas lawmakers give little thought to Bigfoot, but researcher John Lloyd Scharf asked the state's Parks and Wildlife Department for a ruling on Bigfoot hunts in 2012. The noncommittal reply read:

The statute that you cite (Section 61.021) refers only to game birds, game animals, fish, marine animals or other aquatic life. Generally speaking, other nongame wildlife is listed in Chapter 67 (nongame and threatened species) and Chapter 68 (nongame endangered species). "Nongame" means those species of vertebrate and invertebrate wildlife indigenous to Texas that are not classified as game animals, game birds, game fish, fur-bearing animals, endangered species, alligators, marine penaeid shrimp, or oysters. The Parks and Wildlife Commission may adopt regulations to allow a person to take, possess, buy, sell, transport, import, export or propagate nongame wildlife. If the Commission does not specifically list an indigenous, nongame species, then the species is considered non-protected nongame wildlife, e.g., coyote, bobcat, mountain lion, cotton-tailed rabbit, etc. A non-protected nongame animal may be hunted on private property with landowner consent by any means, at any time and there is no bag limit or possession limit.

An exotic animal is an animal that is non-indigenous to Texas. Unless the exotic is an endangered species then exotics may be hunted on private property with landowner consent. A hunting license is required. This does not include the dangerous wild animals that have been held in captivity and released for the purpose of hunting, which is commonly referred to as a "canned hunt."[8]

In short, Lone Star BHMs are fair game.

Not so in New York, where Peter Wiemer of the Chautauqua Lake Bigfoot Expo requested clarification of Bigfoot's status from the state's Department of Environmental Conservation in July 2012. Spokesman Mark Kandel responded three months later, writing that "the DEC does not recognize the occurrence of Big Foot in the state, therefore it is not addressed directly in our hunting regulations. Because it is not addressed there is no open season on Big Foot and they may not be taken."[9]

Body Counts

With or without legal sanction, tales persist of humans killing or attempting to kill hairy bipeds throughout North America. One website lists 218 alleged shooting incidents from thirty-four states and one Canadian province, reported between the late eighteenth century and July 2011. Fifteen of those incidents purportedly ended with dead BHMs. Needless to say—despite one report of a Bigfoot shot and dumped in a well, with its skeleton later recovered—none of those reported slayings left any physical evidence.[10]

Blogger Robert Lindsay offers a different list—or, rather, lists—of Bigfoot kills and captures. His tally includes thirty-seven cases of BHMs killed by humans between 1829 and 2006, eleven live captures reported between the 1820s and 1998, and thirty-three discoveries of possible Bigfoot remains between 1856 and 2008. Those reports span twenty-six US states, plus nine from Canada and one from Mexico.[11]

Accidental Bigfoot kills have also been reported, generally in vague terms or with details that smack of far-flung conspiracy. Robert Lindsay, for example, writes online: "Bigfoots appear to carry off their dead. They are sometimes hit by cars, but in those cases, the Bigfoots usually just ran off after being hit by the cars. In one case, a woman hit a Bigfoot and was killed in the accident. The Bigfoot was also killed. Authorities sealed off the area, and when researchers went back the next day, the body was gone. In the past thirty-five years or so, there are reports of a government coverup regarding dead and injured Bigfoots. Prior to thirty-five years ago, we received no such reports outside the military."[12]

Lindsay also says, "There is also evidence that Bigfoots bury their dead." To support that proposition, he lists nine cases wherein witnesses allegedly observed BHMs conducting funerals, four more discoveries of "possible Bigfoot burial sites" (none of which were excavated), and one incident involving discovery of a dead baby Bigfoot high in a tree. In that case, the Oregon hunter who supposedly found the body "stuck the baby Bigfoot in his deep freeze, and that's the last we've heard of it." Confounding matters further, Lindsay dates the fourteen

Bigfoot conspiracy theories include reports of mysterious black helicopters spiriting away the creatures' corpses. Credit: Author's collection.

incidents from 1949 through 2002, while listing four as "date unknown."[13]

Lindsay's most intriguing report dates from October 1962, when a falling tree allegedly killed a huge female BHM near O'Brien, Oregon. A road crew found the rotting body on November 9. Lindsay writes that "men from a university, along with a logging crew and some locals, took many photos," subsequently confiscated on orders from a US Forest Service district manager. Three days later, Lindsay says, a local ranger "began spreading a lie that the Bigfoot was a pet ape that had escaped from a local residence."[14]

The story might have ended there, but Lindsay takes it further, claiming that the corpse was sent to California, then to Colorado, and then back to California, studied by scientists at each stop. His proof, if we accept it, is "a file on the Bigfoot, USFS/33058-45333-294734-19B," sent with bones and photos to the Smithsonian Institution. From there, the remains and documents moved on to the US Department of the Interior, where everything was "marked classified."[15]

Having thus slammed the door, Lindsay then proceeds to quote from the classified report, as follows:

Species: unknown biped
Date recorded: 3/14/63
Area: O'Brien-Dew Ridge
The bone structure of the specimen is unknown to DGDS
Analyses: Tissue samples indicate non human.

Regarding unknown biped. The subject discussed in the original file is complete with the finding of Dr. D. S. Gould. This is a medical conundrum as to the true species of said subject. Subject appears to be some species not known to date. Some indications are most related to human. Yet many indicate of a gorilla type.

It is noted the length of the subject is clearly not gorilla nor human because subject measurements indicate 98 inches in height. Estimation weight at time of death 770 lbs. This clearly concludes this subject is not consistent with known species of human or gorilla.

Conclusion: Sample is not consistent with any known species of animal/primate known. Seal per request noted.[16]

Lindsay goes on to say that while Forest Service experts "could not figure out what the animal was," Interior Department experts classified it in 1964 "as very similar to an Eastern China Mountain Gorilla."[17] That claim is meaningless on its face, since the only known mountain gorillas (*Gorilla beringei beringei*) inhabit Central Africa. Finally, Lindsay flirts with libel, adding that "some say that this whole story was made up by Linda Newton-Perry [coauthor, with husband Christopher, of the Bigfoot Ballyhoo blog], who is a pathological liar."[18]

The Iceman Cometh, Goeth...and Cometh Back

During 1968-69, showman Frank Hansen toured the North American carnival circuit, hauling a freezer said to contain "The Mysterious Siberskoye Creature," advertised as something "prehistoric." For a quarter each, thousands of gawkers viewed the hairy, vaguely human form within a block of ice, but no eyebrows were raised until December 1968, when Dr. Ivan Sanderson received a phone call at the New Jersey headquarters of his Society for the Investigation of the Unexplained. The caller—herpetologist Terry Cullen, from Minneapolis—had viewed Hansen's exhibit at Chicago's International Livestock Exposition and thought it might be worth a closer look.

Hansen had briefed Cullen on the object's history, and while the details of his story varied from one telling to the next, its essence was as follows: While exhibiting an antique tractor at a fair in Arizona, Hansen was approached by a unnamed "California millionaire" who, in turn, had acquired the frozen body from a wealthy Chinese resident of Hong Kong. Russian sealers allegedly found it floating in a 6,000-pound block of ice, somewhere off Siberia's eastern coast, and sold it on from there. Its American buyer told Hanson:

I'd like to have it exhibited to the public so that they can form their own opinions as to what it might be. I don't want it to be depicted as anything that would upset anyone, but just an interesting sideshow.

I don't want to die and go down in history as the man who upset the biblical version of creation. If you're willing to put up the money yourself to build a show, I'll let you have it for two years.[19]

Hansen jumped at the chance and banked his profits without incident until Sanderson tracked him down, in company with the "father of cryptozoology," Dr. Bernard Heuvelmans of Belgium. Descending on Hansen's farm outside Rollingstone, Minnesota, Sanderson and Heuvelmans examined the body as best they could in its tomb of ice, taking measurements and many photographs between December 16 and 18, 1968. Two months later, Heuvelmans published his "Preliminary Description of the External Morphology of What Appeared to be the Fresh Corpse of a Hitherto Unknown Form of Living Hominid" in the *Bulletin of the Royal Institute of Natural Sciences of Belgium* (Vol. 45, No. 4, February 1969). Sanderson, while working on a scientific paper of his own, initially aired his findings in *Argosy* magazine's May 1969 issue.

That article detailed Sanderson's examination of "a comparatively fresh corpse, preserved in ice, of a specimen of at least one kind of ultra-primitive, fully-haired man-thing, that displays so many heretofore unexpected and non-human characters as to warrant our dubbing it a 'missing link.'" Sanderson professed himself "filled with wonder" at the discovery.[20]

Dubbing the frozen creature "Bozo," he described it as approximately six feet tall, covered in thick hair two to four inches long except on its face, palms, penis, and the soles of its feet. Its shoulders were broad, with "practically no neck," and its hands were "enormous, rather spatulate, but of entirely human proportions" aside from "slender and excessively long" thumbs. Its feet were human in form, without the opposed big toe of great apes. Both eyes had been "blown out," one missing altogether, while the other lay against the creature's cheek. Below a pug nose with large nostrils, two visible teeth resembled those of humans.[21] Sanderson's conclusion:

Let me say, simply, that one look was actually enough to convince us that this was—from our point of view, at least—"the genuine article." This was no phony Chinese trick, or "art" work. If nothing else confirmed this, the appalling stench of rotting flesh exuding from a point in the insulation of the coffin would have been enough...[T]he proportions of this body, and several of its special features, are just not known at all—or, at least, have never been suggested either by paleontologists who have studied the fossil bones of primitive man-things, or even by the skilled artists who have fleshed out and made constructions of what the former have found. In fact, any "artists" setting out to "make" such a thing would have had to have a model, and none is available. But, apart from that, you can't completely fool two trained morphologists with zoological, anatomical and anthropological training. No! Bozo is the genuine article.[22]

Sanderson repeated that endorsement, with more elaborate details, in a scientific paper published on June 18, 1969. Dr. Heuvelmans, meanwhile, was bold enough to proffer a formal scientific name for Hansen's specimen: *Homo pongoides* ("apelike man"). Five years later, the "Minnesota Iceman" served as Exhibit A in Heuvelmans's latest book, *L'homme de Néanderthal est toujours vivant (Neanderthal Man is Still Alive)*. Sadly, despite repeated predictions of its imminent translation, that work remains unavailable in English.

While Heuvelmans labored over his book, Frank Hansen wrote an article for *Saga* magazine—and his story changed radically. Published in July 1970, Hansen's latest version of the Iceman story cast him as the creature's slayer. The thing was not Russian after all, he wrote, but hailed from the vicinity of northern Minnesota's Whiteface Reservoir, where Hansen shot it—in self-defense, of course—in autumn 1960.

As Hansen told the story, he was hunting, following a wounded doe, when he surprised "three hairy creatures" mauling the deer's still-warm carcass. Hansen wrote:

Without warning the male leaped straight into the air from its crouched position. His arms jerked upward, high over his head, and he let out a weird screeching sound. Screeching and screaming, he charged toward me. I cannot remember aiming my rifle nor do I recall pulling the trigger, but a bullet must have slammed into the beast's body.

As blood spurted from his face the huge creature staggered, seemingly stunned by this unexpected happening. I do not recall ejecting my spent shell nor do I recall firing my rifle again. In many sweat-drenched nightmares, however, I have vividly envisioned the blood-covered face lying on the ground beside the mutilated deer. I have absolutely no recollection of ever seeing the other two creatures again. They seemed to have vanished into "thin air."[23]

Horrified, Hansen fled, kept the incident secret, and "spent a month wrestling with my conscience."[24] On December 2, 1960, he returned to the shooting site and found the creature dead, half buried in snow. Fearing legal repercussions, Hansen says he hauled the body home and stashed it in cold storage, since frozen ground precluded grave digging. He planned to bury it in spring but changed his mind, and after his retirement from the Air Force, Hansen hit the road with his trophy to relieve the drudgery of farming.

Life was sweet and profitable until Sanderson and Heuvelmans arrived on Hansen's doorstep and revealed his secret to the world. Fortunately, Hansen

Frank Hansen's public story, claiming that he killed the "Minnesota Iceman." Credit: Author's collection.

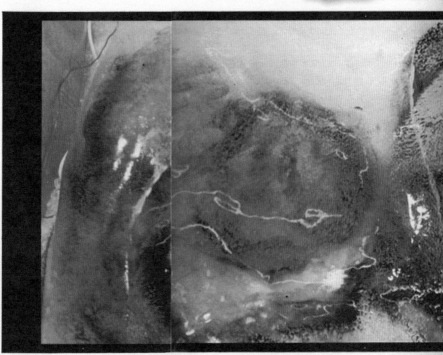

For years the "thing" has been exhibited in carny sideshows and state fairs around the U.S. and in Canada.
For years the "monster" has been the subject of a bitter feud between its owner and government agencies.
For years the "specimen" has fueled a raging battle among scientists—is it an incredible hoax or a fantastic anthropological find? Now, for the first time anywhere, the man responsible for the biggest controversy to hit the scientific world in the past decade presents his own story to the public, and leaves it to the reader to decide if it's

FACT or
FICTION

I KILLED THE
APE-MAN CREATURE OF WHITEFACE

By Frank Hansen
Copyright 1970 by Frank Hansen

wrote in *Saga*, he had taken the precaution of commissioning a life-size model of his trophy in advance, before he started touring, and in the hectic spring of 1969 he switched the bodies, on advice from his attorney, spreading word that its wealthy owner had demanded the creature's return. After touring a while longer with the fake corpse, billed as "a fabricated illusion," Hansen retired the model and went back to showing antique tractors at fairs.25

There matters rested until June 2013, when Steve Busti—owner of the Museum of the Weird in Austin, Texas—purchased the "original" Iceman from Hansen's estate. Two years of research had convinced Busti that Hansen told the truth in *Saga* four decades earlier. "He shot it in Wisconsin," Busti told the Huffington Post. "Its eyeball's blown out and its arm is broken. I couldn't believe it had been in Minnesota the entire time."26

Neither could skeptics, who continue to dismiss the icebound relic as a fraud.

"Bugs" Meets Bigfoot

On April 16, 1996, Art Bell's Nevada-based paranormal radio talk show received a call from a man identified as "Bugs," claiming that he and two companions shot a pair of BHMs, male and female in 1976, while hunting in Maverick County, Texas, near the Mexican border. Fearing possible prosecution, the shooters buried their kills in unmarked graves and kept quiet about the incident until Bugs broke cover twenty years later. Curiously—unlike every other primate known to science—both dead BHMs reportedly had six toes on each foot.

Bugs continued to grace Bell's show through the turn of the century appearing once with researcher Robert Morgan (who seemed to find his story credible), and he was featured on YouTube until the interview was removed "due to multiple third-party notifications of copyright infringement."27 Craig Woolheater spoke for most researchers when he wrote, in October 2007, "I for one am not going to go to the Elm Creek area of Texas to dig four to five foot deep for twenty-five-year-old bones of a hairy six-toed goliath and his female counterpart, but perhaps someone might."28

To date, no one has.

Dead and Gone?

T hus far, the twenty-first century has produced six significant claims of Bigfoot kills from five states. One of those stories is a "flashback" to 1967, included here because it first made news in 2009. Two reports describe killings of multiple BHMs. Taking the tales in order of revelation, we begin in far-southeastern Oklahoma with "the Siege of Honobia."

In mid-January 2000 the BFRO received its first message from a family living outside Honobia, Oklahoma, describing two years of harassment by BHMs that climaxed in violence. The "victims" of the siege had planted snow peas on their property, attracting deer that they hunted for food year-round, without much regard for legality. Problems arose when the deer attracted monsters with a taste for venison and no fear of humans, leading to a "siege" complete with doorknob rattling, window scratching, and thefts of meat from an outdoor freezer. Days before contacting the BFRO, farmer "Tim" allegedly blasted one BHM with an assault rifle, afterward finding a broad trail of blood but no trace of a body.

At that point, a BFRO investigator from Ohio flew to the scene, hoping to collect forensic evidence. Alas, as he reported:

There is a trail of blood in the woods, but it leads to the fresh deer kill, not away from the area where the bigfoot was standing when he fired at it. Tim says the Bigfoot ran after he shot at it, but then he and his brother could hear it and others on the hillside for several hours after the shooting. That suggests to me that he didn't even wound it, and all the blood is from the deer.[29]

More investigators came, reporting nocturnal encounters and sporadic gunfire, none of it producing either physical or photographic evidence. By the time blogger Robert Lindsay told the tale in May 2011, it sounded more like Ape Canyon in 1924.

That night, the Bigfoots came around again, and all Hell broke loose. The male family members and the BFRO guys were all armed. They spent most of the night spotlighting the woods and shooting at the Bigfoots. The Bigfoots threw rocks and screamed and carried on. They seemed to have lost their fear of guns and spotlights because they had seen the family spotlighting deer so much that they did not associate guns with harm, because all the guns ever did was shoot deer. At one point, a Bigfoot was apparently shot and killed, but the other Bigfoots came to grab the body and retreated with it. After that, the problem was pretty much taken care of, and the Bigfoots stopped harassing the people.[30]

That garbled recitation of events bears no resemblance to the BFRO's on-site report, leaving Lindsay to add a gratuitous footnote. "About half of the organization left after this," he wrote. "Afterward, Matt Moneymaker turned the BFRO into a glorified Bigfoot tour guide focusing on $2,000 expeditions into the woods to go looking for Bigfoots."[31]

"No Comment"

In October 2001, Montana's *Billings Gazette* reported rumors of a Bigfoot killing and its cover-up by federal officials. According to the newspaper, "The stories have been circulating for three months. In most, the beast was killed near the Crow Reservation and its corpse was zipped into a body bag and whisked away by federal agents minutes before local authorities could investigate." Spokesmen for Montana Fish, Wildlife and Parks made a joke of the stories, while the state's top FBI agent assured reporters that "we are not doing anything covertly to hide a body. I do not have a Bigfoot in my evidence locker."[32] —which, of course, is exactly what participants in a conspiracy would say!

The alleged triggerman, Pryor Creek rancher Steve Kukowski, also did his best to stifle rumors that he shot a BHM for terrorizing his livestock. "The rumors have been going around all summer," he told the *Gazette*. "I have no idea what it is. I have no idea how it got started."[33]

And there, until a body surfaces, the matter rests.

Avenging Abby

On November 14, 2003, Loren Coleman reported that "something important may have happened" in Campbell County, Tennessee. According to Coleman, a female goat named Abby was found dead in a pond at LaFollette on November 10, its neck broken and its stomach "eaten out." Two days later, Coleman wrote, "Sirens and gunshots were heard. Screams of the recently sighted apelike animals were also heard at the same time." On November 13 an anonymous member of the county sheriff's department allegedly remarked "that they were working with a group to eliminate these animals."[34]

Local researcher/habituator Mary Green added claims that a rogue BHM had killed "many" cats, in addition to Abby, before police intervened. While the cats' owners prepared to flee, Green wrote, "The Sheriff and his deputies were heavily involved with shooting over the hill just off of their property. This morning [November 14]...the woman saw a black animal laying in one of their fields. She called me before she left for work as she was running late. I advised her to get her husband to take a look at this animal. He arrived ten minutes after she left and the animal was totally missing. Gone. Nothing left, not a sign of it. Nothing was found. There has [sic] been airplanes circling their property night and day for over two weeks. It has disturbed their sleep as the plane was flying so low to their house."[35]

Sophisticated cover-up, or flight of fantasy? For those who call Ms. Green a crackpot, there is no debate. Elsewhere, the argument persists.

Requiem for Chiye-tanka

Loren Coleman also broke the next report of a BHM killing—this one from South Dakota's Pine Ridge Reservation—on August 6, 2006. While skeptical, he offered a posting from the *Godlike Productions* blog, a self-described forum on "UFOs, Conspiracy Theorists, [and the] Lunatic Fringe."[36] That anonymous post read as follows, without corrections:

There is a trail of blood in the woods, but it leads to the fresh deer kill, not away from the area where the bigfoot was standing when it fired at it. Tim says the Bigfoot ran after he shot at it, but then he and his brother could hear it and others on the hillside for several hours after the shooting. That suggests to me that he didn't even wound it, and all the blood is from the deer.[29]

I just talked to my sister in law who's on the Pine Ridge Reservation. She said that last Tuesday night [August 1] supposedly someone shot and killed a bigfoot near the Slim Buttes area. This is basically insider gossip, as there is no way to verify it. But, she said that several medicine men including Wilmer Mesteth, Oliver Red Cloud and Tom (?) Janis were called over there by the police to the site, and they smudged the body with burning sage and cedar, and said prayers. (The lakota see the bigfoot as a sort of spirit being, and are scared of it.) Anyway, then it was wrapped up and taken to the lab at the School of Mines in Rapid City. All kind of hush hush, but this is the inside gossip. I have no way to verify it, but my sister in law has never lied to me. She said she doesn't know if it's true as she hasn't spoken to anyone who actually saw it. But I just thought you would be interested to hear the rumors.[37]

Five years after the alleged event, Robert Lindsay confused matters further, writing: "A Bigfoot that had been named Chiye-tanka was shot and killed on the reservation. It was later given to the School of Mines to study. They sent it back, and it was given a ceremonial burial by Lakota elders. Government coverup."[38] Lindsay credits the tale to Ray Crowe, a longtime Bigfoot researcher whose vast archives logged fantastic claims of BHM kills and captures alongside relatively "normal" sightings. Sadly, since those archives were removed from the Internet in 2008, no public review of Crowe's claims on this case is possible.

South Dakota's Pine Ridge Indian Reservation, scene of much violence against humans...and Bigfoot?
Credit: US National Park Service.

Patty Whacked?

The most surprising—many say incredible—report of a BHM killing surfaced in May 2008, when researcher M. K. Davis floated a theory that female Sasquatch "Patty" was not only filmed by Roger Patterson in October 1967, but was also gunned down, with several others of her species, in what came to be called "the Bluff Creek Massacre." As the "theory" evolved, with Bob Gimlin cast as the primary triggerman, Davis claimed to see and hear things in the original jerky film clip that had eluded viewers for decades: braids and a topknot on Patty, a "bloody leg," baying hounds, and lurking men with "red hands" who presumably slaughtered the hapless party of bipeds or, at the very least, joined in their burial.

From there, the rumor mill took over, painting a scenario with backhoes summoned to dig a mass grave for the slain gentle giants, while venerable researchers John Green and Bob Titmus joined in the forty-year cover-up. Roused to comment in August 2009, Green replied that the "Patterson footage" used by Davis to make his case was, in fact, a film shot by René Dahinden at a wholly different place and time. He concluded:

I can't think up any time line that could make sense and haven't encountered anyone else's explanation of it. It appears that I am supposed to have heard of the massacre somehow and taken the tracking dog to try to find the site, then having found it having joined in the conspiracy to cover it up. That would get me there while there was still red blood all around, but would have to be after the actual shooting and before Patterson and Gimlin buried anything—but Patterson's movie has to have been made after the burying to raise the level of the ground. The more I try to explain the stranger it seems that anyone could think this stuff up, let alone actually go public with it, let alone have anyone else believe it.[39]

Hours after Green's denial appeared online, Davis removed his video clips from YouTube, though selected frames may still be viewed on the Cryptomundo website.[40] Nothing has surfaced in the interim to lend his theory further credence.

Bigfoot Steak

n November 2010, native Texan Justin Smeja visited the website Taxidermy. net, announcing that he had killed two BHMs and seeking advice from blog readers. From there, as Robert Lindsay reports, the thread spun out of control until site moderators got wind of threats against Smeja, finally shutting it down.[41] That move came too late, as the story went viral, mutating on its passage through the Internet rumor mill. Five years later, with the dust fairly settled, we may summarize the "facts" as follows:

Smeja and a friend were hunting for bear near Gold Lake, in California's Plumas National Forest (Butte County), when they saw a female Bigfoot advancing toward their vehicle. Despite his driver's warning not to fire, suggesting that the creature was "a man in a monkey suit," Smeja shot it in the chest, then trailed the dying creature to a brushy area where it collapsed beside two juvenile specimens. Smeja killed one of them, in turn, but the other escaped when Smeja's furious partner snatched the rifle from his hands. Finally realizing that the animals were not bears, Smeja left them where they lay and fled the area with his companion.

Enter the Olympic Project, led by Derek Randles, seeking proof of Bigfoot's existence. After long talks with Smeja, Randles declared, "I completely believe him."[42] He also persuaded Smeja to retrieve flesh samples from the BHMs in July 2011, for DNA testing. According to Randles:

Upon returning they were greeted with roughly two feet of snow. The little one was not found. They concentrated their efforts in the area where they thought they heard the larger one go down. After digging through the snow for many hours they were able to find a piece of flesh, greasy fat and hair, but no body. The flesh and hair matched the color of the larger one exactly. White gray hair with some black in it.[43]

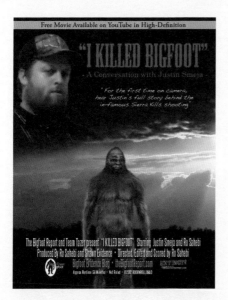

Free Movie Available on YouTube in High-Definition

"I KILLED BIGFOOT"
- A Conversation with Justin Smeja -

'For the first time on camera, hear Justin's full story behind the infamous Sierra Kills shooting'

The Bigfoot Report and Team Tazer present "I KILLED BIGFOOT" Starring Justin Smeja and Ro Sahebi
Produced By Ro Sahebi and Shawn Evidence · Directed, Edited and Scored by Ro Sahebi
Bigfoot Evidence Blog · theBigfootReport.com

Justin Smeja's video, promoting
the unsupported tale that he
killed two Bigfoot creatures in
2010. Credit: Author's collection.

Urged on by Randles, Smeja sent the "Bigfoot steak"—Robert Lindsay's description—to Dr. Melba Ketchum (see Chapter 5) for DNA sequencing. The results of that test are muddled by contradictory reports. According to Robert Lindsay, "The Bigfoot steak tests out as 'no known mammal.' However, the DNA tests as 'human.'"[44] Blogger Joe Black, posting to The Bigfoot Field Journal online, disagrees, stating that two separate labs identified Smeja's sample as containing black bear DNA with human contamination. Based on that and other factors, Black calls Smeja's story a hoax.[45]

But was Black correct?

In August 2012, the *Bigfoot Evidence* blog told readers that Smeja had submitted to testing by "one of Sacramento's top polygraph examiners" and passed with flying colors. More specifically, the unnamed examiner asked seventeen questions written by Bart Cutino—named by Joe Black as a party to the Smeja hoax—and Smeja answered each in turn with "no deception indicated." The anonymous blogger went on to write: "To our knowledge, the type of polygraph we chose cannot be faked. It has a ninety-nine percent accuracy and it uses the same technique used by the military. Justin passed 100 percent."[46]

Without judging Smeja's veracity, we may say with assurance that the blogger's view of polygraphs is badly skewed. Thirty-one US states exclude "lie detector" tests from admission as evidence in court, while nineteen allow admission only if both sides in a trial agree. Polygraphs measure pulse, respiration, and skin conductivity (sweating), not honesty, and they may be defeated by countermeasures ranging from drugs to meditation and hypnosis. CIA traitor Aldrich Ames dismissed the agency's regular polygraph tests as "witch-doctory," adding, "there's no special magic" to beating the machine. "Confidence is what does it," Ames said. "Confidence and a friendly relationship with the examiner...rapport, where you smile and you make him think that you like him."[47]

On a personal note, I have been tested on polygraphs twice, six years apart and by different operators in different cities, hired by different employers. Each test returned false results—an error factor of 100 percent in my case.

Lost in
Translation

t 10:30 a.m. on May 14, 2013, the following radio exchange occurred between a police officer in Altoona, Pennsylvania, and his dispatcher. A transcript of the brief, slightly garbled transmission reads:

Dispatcher: Mr. Winesickle, 97 Spruce Street?
Officer: Negative
Dispatcher: He called 911 advising that he contacted the Game Commission. They haven't called him back. He wants a police officer to come to his residence. Apparently he has proof there of Bigfoot.

Officer: Bigfoot, right?
Dispatcher: That's affirmative. He has evidence proving Bigfoot. He would like a police officer to come there.
Officer: Apparently there's a large amount of smoke in that area.[48]

Static ends the exchange, but that was not the end of the story. At 2:41 p.m. the Pennsylvania Bigfoot Society (PBS) received an e-mail from a ham radio operator, reading:

Today in Somerset County, PA, a turkey hunter shot and killed an animal he claimed is a Sasquatch. The state police were called and responded to the scene, according to chatter on the local police frequencies the officers confirmed there was an unidentified animal shot and killed. Details are a bit fuzzy at this time. Any investigative assistance would be appreciated.[49]

Another e-mail, including the ham operator's name and phone number, followed at 3:20 p.m. It read, in part:

Hello, YES this is legit, a strange report came over the scanner here in Somerset, Pa. just a few miles from Flight 93 memorial. The message went to the local Police department. The report stated that a hunter had shot a Sasquatch while hunting turkey this morning. This is the first day of Spring Turkey [hunting season] in Pennsylvania. Later a second confirmation message on the scanner stated that yes there was a body but was unable to identify who or what it was. This all started about 10:30 AM and continued through most of the day. The location was stated as Russell or Rustic Road (too fast to be sure) here in the local area of Somerset County, Pennsylvania. Just wanted to let someone know.[50]

Referring to witness John Winesickle, the e-mail continued:

What he said he heard was that a hunter had called and stated that he had shot a Bigfoot. He soon heard some radio chatter from police who were reportedly joking about the report. It was about twenty minutes later that he said he heard a police officer radio back and state, 'there was a body.

Soon after that, Winesickle heard a helicopter approaching. According to the e-mail:

The sound was so loud it shook his house, so he went outside to take a look. It was then that he observed a formation of four Army Apache helicopters approaching from the north and moving in the direction of Somerset.[51]

PBS investigator Ron Gallucci contacted the ham operator, followed shortly by veteran UFO/Bigfoot researcher Stan Gordon. Gallucci next called Somerset's State Police Barracks, discovering that Winesickle had reported finding Bigfoot tracks on his rural property, but claimed no sighting. An officer had responded and photographed footprints that he (the officer) thought had been made by a bear.

Meanwhile, still on May 14, PBS director Eric Altman accessed a website that archives radio transmissions from police, firefighters, emergency medical services, aircraft, and trains.[52] Downloading the relevant broadcasts, he found no mention of a Bigfoot sighting, much less a BHM shooting. By May 15, Stan Gordon had denials in hand from the Pennsylvania Game Commission. On May 16, Paint Township's chief of police made it unanimous, stating that officers had been dispatched to Winesickle's home "on an animal complaint issue of an individual claiming to find large Bigfoot tracks in the forest."[53] They found two sets of footprints, one smaller than the other, suggesting an adult bear with a cub.

What of the roaring helicopters? Eric Altman learned that the Pennsylvania Army National Guard flies frequent training missions with Apache helicopters out of nearby John Murtha-Johnstown-Cambria County Airport. The unit's commanding officer denied any knowledge of a Bigfoot corpse retrieval—which, again, is what we might expect from a conspirator.

Let John Winesickle have the final word. Speaking to reporters from Altoona's WTAJ-TV, he denied any Bigfoot sighting or shooting, while claiming that he "once came close" to spotting the creature. "It's deathly afraid,' he explained. "It won't hurt you."[54]

What of the bear tracks? "No, no," Winesickle insisted. "A bear can't go down a steep bank on all twos. This is Bigfoot. The police have been very nice to me. It wasn't a bear, it was Bigfoot."[55]

But alas, once more, no proof.

CHAPTER 5

SASQUATCH CSI

If hunters never kill or capture Bigfoot, is there any other way to prove that BHMs exit?

Perhaps. Despite widespread disdain for "circumstantial" evidence, there have been secured convictions in countless criminal cases, often where the stakes are life or death, with a guilty verdict demanding certainty "beyond reasonable doubt." What are the net results, if we apply such evidence to Bigfoot and its kin?

Is Seeing Believing?

What weight does anecdotal evidence—descriptions of events from one or more eyewitnesses—carry with mainstream science? The answer we must recognize is "virtually none."

In court, eyewitness testimony pleases jurors, but judges, lawyers, and police know that such testimony, even given under oath, is often unreliable. Witnesses make mistakes, particularly under stress or in unfamiliar surroundings. Some lie deliberately; others may be mentally impaired. In the worst-case scenario, authorities may suppress exculpatory testimony, while presenting only witnesses who aid the prosecution's case. Since 1977, at least thirty American death row inmates have been exonerated by scientific methods unknown at the time they were sentenced to die. Many more have had their prison terms commuted, sometimes after serving decades behind bars.

Bigfoot skeptics are correct in saying that eyewitness accounts—ranging from relatively "mundane" to radically bizarre—are insufficient to establish the existence of a species presently unrecognized by science. Those same skeptics overstep, however, in suggesting that all witnesses must be mistaken, lying, or mentally incompetent based on a preconception that Bigfoot does not exist.

No one doubts that footprints have been faked, that pranksters have disguised themselves as monsters, or that garden-variety liars have fabricated Bigfoot sightings, either to amuse themselves or in a bid for notoriety. In Chapter 6 we shall discuss a wide variety of Bigfoot hoaxes. Consider, though, the scope of the conspiracy involved if every Bigfoot witness was a hoaxer, not only in America, but all around the world, receding back into the mists of time.

That leap of faith—and it is nothing less for skeptics, never mind their claim to be hard-headed rationalists who demand full proof of any allegation—brings us inevitably to the situation faced in 2002, when track hoaxer Ray Wallace died in Washington State. Wallace was barely cold before his kinfolk, seeking fame and fortune, claimed that he "invented" Bigfoot and that "Bigfoot died" with him. The media swallowed that fable without pausing to consider how a man born in 1918, confined for most of his life to the Pacific Northwest, could have "invented" global sightings dating back to ancient times.

Suffice it here to say that anecdotal evidence must be approached with caution and a healthy, honest skepticism that does not assume solutions to a riddle in advance. Beyond that, we are left to look for other forms of proof.

Picture Perfect?

ountless felons are imprisoned today because they were caught red-handed on film or on videotape. An abysmally stupid subset of that number videotape their own crimes for personal entertainment, and the really stupid ones post those tapes online. Needless to say, they are amazed when judges sentence them to jail.

While society debates the efficacy and morality of widespread video surveillance over daily life, we turn our attention to photos, films, and videos purporting to depict wild BHMs. And it should come as no surprise that a purported Bigfoot caught on film or tape is not at all the same thing as a felon taped while burglarizing shops or stealing cars.

I'm personally unaware of any videos or photos introduced at trial in the United States, which proved to be fakes. It may have happened, but if so, I

One of many anonymous hoax photos, pretending to depict a Bigfoot killed by hunters. Credit: Author's collection.

missed the bulletin. "Monsters," by contrast, normally appear to witnesses at some remote location, or at least in situations where official cameras are not installed. In bygone days, most hikers, hunters, and the like did not pack photographic gear into the wilderness, but now, when every cell phone has a built-in camera, no heavy special gear is needed.

Sadly, the advances of technology also make faking photographs and videos much simpler than it was in days of yore. As Adobe Photoshop and its competitors are used to spruce up fashion models, scenery—most anything at all—so they assist hoaxers in pulling off a wide range of amusing or malicious pranks. Your face might be excised from the most innocent photograph, transplanted to the worst frames of a squalid child-porn video. You may have spent your whole life in the desert, yet appear in realistic surfing footage, chased by giant sharks.

The possibilities are virtually endless.

The first purported still photo of Bigfoot was published by the *San Francisco Chronicle* on December 14, 1965, five years after woodsman Zack Hamilton left the undeveloped film at a local camera shop and never returned. Nine years later, Ohio tourist Rosemary Tobash snapped a photo of something in British Columbia's Kootenay National Park. Still photos have multiplied over the years, ranging from blurry "Squatchblobs" to crystal-clear shots derided by many observers as fakes. Thus far, no still photo of any quality has swayed the mind of mainstream science from denial to acceptance of live BHMs.

The best-known Bigfoot film released for public scrutiny—many would say the most persuasive evidence to date—remains Roger Patterson's Bluff Creek film from 1967 (see Chapter 1). Still intensely controversial, despite the passage of nearly four decades, the film is viewed by some researchers as a kind of Holy Grail, supported by no end of books and articles discussing "Patty's" height, weight, stride, and attitude. Skeptics, meanwhile, stake their knee-jerk denial on "confessions" from at least three different Patty impersonators, coupled with furious insistence that Bigfoot is "impossible."

A brief online investigation will reveal scores, if not hundreds, of supposed Bigfoot video clips on YouTube and other video hosting sites, posted from around the world (see Chapter 8). Quality varies radically, perhaps by design, and some of the clearest frames are frankly laughable. As matters stand today, no footage, in and of itself, is viewed by mainstream scientists as proof of anything.

Best Impressions

Bigfoot was named for its huge, humanoid footprints, commonly reported as being fifteen to eighteen inches long and six to nine inches wide. Compare that to a man's size 16 shoe in the United States, which measures

12½ inches long. The largest man on record, Robert Wardlow of Illinois, wore a size 37AA shoe, 18.5 inches long. He also stood eight feet, eleven inches tall and weighed 435 pounds, more than a fair approximation of the average Bigfoot described by eyewitnesses.

No one, of course, suggests that Wardlow was Bigfoot. Born in 1918, like Ray Wallace, Wardlow spent most of his life in the public eye, requiring leg braces to stand by the time he died in 1940 at age twenty-two. At least sixteen other men and one woman—Zeng Jinlian of China—have topped the eight-foot mark, encroaching into Bigfoot territory.[1]

Footprint discoveries far outnumber eyewitness sightings of live BHMs nationwide. In many cases, only one print is discovered—or, worse yet, a partial print—in some remote location where it seems unlikely that a hoaxer would expect to find a sucker passing by. Other sites reveal trackways extending over a protracted distance. One such find, from Washington State, also revealed what some researchers describe as the best evidence of Bigfoot's existence.

The tale begins with Ivan Marx. In 1959, at thirty-eight, he joined a Bigfoot expedition organized and funded by Texas oilman Tom Slick, veteran of four prior efforts to find Yetis in the Himalayas. Other members of the team included zoologist/author Ivan Sanderson, Peter Byrne, taxidermist Robert Titmus, and René Dahinden. Bigfoot remained elusive, while dissension racked the team. Loren Coleman writes that Marx's behavior was "one of the major reasons that René Dahinden decided to leave the California search and go back to Canada." John Green, around the same time, labeled Marx "the biggest, well, yarn-spinner in California."[2]

In 1969, Marx moved to Bossburg, in the far northeast corner of Washington State. On November 24 of that year, butcher Joseph Rhodes of Colville found Bigfoot tracks—the first of many to appear over the next few months—near Bossburg's dump. Unlike prior footprints found worldwide, the right foot in this series was deformed, as if it had been broken and the bones had healed leaving the toes off-center, pointing inward. Word of "Cripple Foot" soon spread, drawing researchers and tourists alike, while countless other tracks appeared in the vicinity. One trail, examined by René Dahinden and Dr. Grover Krantz on December 13, included 1,089 distinct footprints meandering through the forest and across roads, stepping over a forty-three-inch-high, five-strand wire fence, elsewhere "skiing" down slopes with one foot used as a brake.[3]

None of the many searchers sighted Cripple Foot, but the evidence it left behind encouraged them. The prowler's left foot measured 17½ inches long, 6½ inches across the ball, and 5½ inches across the heel. Its right, with the deformity, measured 16½ inches long, seven inches across the ball, and 5½ inches across the heel. Dr. Krantz later wrote that the tracks were "right on. Such an animal would have had to walk exactly as this one did: stride, angle of foot placement, distribution of weight—it was all exactly as it had to be. Before I examined these prints, I would have given you ten-to-one odds that the whole thing was a hoax. But there is no way that everything could have been tied together so perfectly in a fake."[4]

Skeptic John Napier, a British physician, primatologist and paleoanthropologist, likewise accepted the tracks as genuine, writing:

Apart from satisfying the criteria established for modern human-type walking, the Bossburg prints have, to my way of thinking, an even greater claim to authenticity. The right foot of the Bossburg Sasquatch is a club-foot, a not uncommon abnormality....The forepart of the foot is twisted inwards, the third toe has been squeezed out of normal alignment, and possibly there has been a dislocation of the bones on the outer border (but this last feature may be due to an imperfection in the casting technique). Club-foot usually occurs as a congenital abnormality, but it may also develop as the result of severe injury, or of damage to the nerves controlling the muscle of the foot. To me the deformity strongly suggests that injury during life was responsible. A true, untreated, congenital (club-foot) usually results in a fixed flexion deformity of the ankle in which case only the forepart of the foot and toes touch the ground in normal standing. In these circumstances the heel impression would be absent or poorly defined; but in fact the heel indentation of the Sasquatch is strongly defined. I conclude that the deformity was the result of a crushing injury to the foot during early childhood. It is very difficult to conceive of a hoaxer so subtle, so knowledgeable—and so sick—who would deliberately fake a footprint of this nature. I suppose it is possible, but it is so unlikely that I am prepared to discount it.[5]

In October 1970, Ivan Marx phoned René Dahinden, claiming to have a film of "the cripple," photographed seven miles north of Bossburg. The creature on screen appeared to be injured—allegedly after colliding with a car or train (reports varied)—but despite the film's "extreme clarity," it revealed no facial features. Even when the subject turned to glare at Marx, it remained a large black silhouette. John Green, despite his judgment of Marx as a champion "yarn-spinner," told the *Bigfoot Bulletin*, "I am satisfied...that he could not have faked all he has to show, and that the film is genuine."[6]

That confidence faded over time, as Marx announced more Bigfoot finds: footprints, handprints, and new film footage, finally collected in 1976 for the theatrical release of his documentary, *The Legend of Bigfoot* (see Chapter 6). Today, some skeptics claim Marx faked the "cripple" tracks. Others blame confessed hoaxer Ray Pickens, whose clumsy wooden feet, attached to work boots, bear no resemblance to the "cripple's" tracks. Confusing matters further, Pickens has admitted that he carved his first fake feet in 1971.[7] Loren Coleman provides the story's epitaph:

A replica of the Mill Creek "Wrinkle Foot" cast. Credit: Author's collection.

After Cripple Foot, in 1982, came "Wrinkle Foot," whose prints were found and cast by researcher Paul Freeman at the Mill Creek watershed in Oregon's Blue Mountains. Examination of the casts appeared to reveal dermal ridges (*cristae cutis*), which are "produced by the projecting papillae of the dermis on the palm of the hand or sole of the foot, producing a fingerprint or footprint characteristic of the individual."[9] Found only on the palms and soles of primates, those ridges might not only prove specific tracks legitimate, but also might—at least in theory—permit researchers to track a specific primate in its ramblings.

Dr. Grover Krantz was quick to call the Mill Creek casts the best proof yet of Bigfoot's existence, writing:

Thus far, every specialist who has examined these casts agrees that their detailed anatomy has all the characteristics and appearance of being derived from an imprint of primate skin. These now include thirty police fingerprint workers, mostly from the Western states, twelve of whom might be considered experts. Also included are six physical anthropologists with expertise in this area, as well as four pathologists and two zoologists. At present, two of the police experts are willing to state categorically that the prints actually represent the existence of a real but unknown animal, regardless of the implications.... Even the strongest critic, a mammalogist at the Smithsonian Institution, agrees that the casts represent primate skin, but he thinks that it must have been transferred from known animals by silicone rubber casting and combined somehow to form the tracks.[10]

Opposing those experts were René Dahinden and Robert Titmus, whose unsupported opinions naturally carried more weight with journals such as the *Skeptical Inquirer*. In 1993, Dahinden allegedly told SI reporter Michael Dennett, "Look, any village idiot can see those tracks are fake, 100 percent fake!" Titmus agreed, ranking Freeman's casts (and alleged Bigfoot handprints he later discovered) as "probably the worst evidence for Bigfoot." Freeman did not help his case when, in 1987, he admitted that he tried to fake Bigfoot tracks before finding the "real" ones at Mill Creek.[11]

Meanwhile, fingerprint experts John Berry and Stephen Haylock examined the casts, reporting that:

The dermal ridges present appear to us of 'normal' type and size and not larger than one would expect on any human or ape hand or foot. Sweat pores also appear and these too are normally spaced along the ridge summits. The difference between the pores and bubbles in the latex-casting medium can easily be distinguished....Together, these casts appear to represent the foot of a highly unusual creature, flatfooted in the extreme and with a congenital disorder—ridge dissociation." They conclude that the casts might be fakes, but if so, "the 'culprit' is worthy of the Lewis Minshall Award [issued annually by the Fingerprint Society to members who make outstanding contributions in their field].[12]

Flash forward to September 2000, in Washington's Gifford Pinchot National Forest. While filming an episode of the *Animal X* television series (see Chapter 8), a ten-member BFRO expedition found three "potential" Bigfoot tracks—one seventeen inches long—and recorded loud "answers" to call-blasting on September 20, then discovered "an unusual impression in the transition mud at the edge of [a] muddy pool area" two days later. As described in an October press release, the impression seemed to be made by "a large animal's left forearm, hip, thigh, and heel."[13]

The team made a plaster cast of the imprint, measuring sixty by forty inches, weighing more than 200 pounds, and transported it to the Idaho State University lab of Dr. Jeffrey Meldrum. According to the school's press agent:

The investigating team, including Meldrum; Dr. Grover Krantz...; Dr. John Bindernagel, ...; John Green...; and Dr. Ron Brown, exotic animal handler and health care administrator, all examined the cast and agreed that it cannot be attributed to any commonly known Northwest animal and may represent an unknown primate.

After the cast was cleaned, extensive impressions of hair on the buttock and thigh surfaces and a fringe of longer hair along the forearm were evident. Meldrum identified what appear to be skin ridge patterns on the heel, comparable to fingerprints, that are characteristic of primates.

The ridge characteristics are consistent with other examples from Sasquatch footprints Meldrum has studied....The anatomy of the heel, ankle, and Achilles tendon are also distinct and consistent with models of the Sasquatch foot derived by Meldrum after examining hundreds of alleged Sasquatch footprints.

Hair samples collected at the scene and from the cast itself and examined by Dr. Henner Fahrenbach, a biomedical research scientist from Beaverton, Ore., were primarily of deer, elk, coyote, and bear, as was expected since tracks in the wallow were mostly of those animals. However, based on characteristics matching those of otherwise indeterminate primate hairs collected in association with other Sasquatch sightings, he identified a single distinctly primate hair as "Sasquatch."[14]

Encouraged, Meldrum said, "While not definitively proving the existence of a species of North American ape, the cast constitutes significant and compelling new evidence that will hopefully stimulate further serious research and investigation into the presence of these primates in the Northwest mountains and elsewhere."[15] John Green added:

A replica of the controversial Skookum cast.
Credit: Author's collection.

For more than forty years I have held the opinion that science can not be convinced of the existence of Sasquatches by anything less than physical remains. I have now changed my opinion. I think the Skookum cast can do it, provided that enough influential zoologists, mammalogists, anatomists, primatologists, etc. will take a serious look at it. The evidence that this imprint was made by a very large, unknown, higher primate is, in my opinion, compelling. I would not anticipate that every qualified person who examines [it] would come to the same conclusion, but I feel sure that the vast majority would have to, whatever their preconceptions.[16]

Alas, he was mistaken. Few mainstream experts bothered looking at the cast, and critics of the BFRO team's analysis, ranging from *Skeptical Inquirer* to longtime BFRO adversary Cliff Crook, loudly proclaimed the cast an imprint of a reclining elk's body. Crook—blasted in BFRO editorials online as a perennial hoaxer[17]—delighted in ridiculing the Skookum cast, publicly dubbing it "Spoofem."[18] Canadian reporter Marc Hume also claimed to recognize the cast as "imprints left that would match perfectly with an elk's legs."[19]

Tantalizing finds continue to the present day. Shortly before his death in 2008, researcher Mike Sells cast a handprint found in sandy soil near Paris, Texas. The print measured 12½ inches long, suggesting that its owner should stand roughly ten feet tall.[20] The grainy soil prevented observation of small dermal ridges, but Internet reporter David Claerr writes "that creases in the palm (also referred to as 'life lines' in palmistry) are fairly distinct."[21] Claerr also broke the news of another Texas find in May 2012. Specifically:

A very significant group of footprints of a "Baby Bigfoot" were cast in plaster, along with a hand- and footprints from a more mature Sasquatch, most likely the juvenile's older sibling or mother. The prints, pressed into the fine clay of the creek bed are rare specimens, since not only are they from a rarely documented young juvenile, but the casts also retain detailed anatomical features that are not generally preserved in other types of soil.[22]

Sadly, no further information is available beyond Claerr's personal judgment that the "baby" print "is most likely from a juvenile that would be equivalent to a human 'toddler'...who has just begun to walk upright....The accompanying footprints are of an individual, most likely female, probably about six foot [*sic*] tall, small for an adult female and possibly indicating an older sibling."[23] Claerr offers no clue as to how sex or age may be judged from the larger footprints.

Collateral
Damage

Foot- and handprints are not the only traces linked by researchers to BHMs. Reports persist that hairy bipeds twist and break trees, build beds or nests, leave mutilated carcasses of wildlife and domestic animals, and damage humans' property, either by accident or otherwise.

Breakage or twisting of trees was linked to Bigfoot long before the first Europeans trespassed on North America. At least five different tribes in the Pacific Northwest—the Colville, Klickitat, Puyallup, Twana, and Yakama peoples—used names for BHMs that whites translated as meaning "stick Indians."[24] John Green adds a story reported two years before "Bigfoot" made its premiere at Bluff Creek.

Finally, there is a story published in *Sports Afield* in 1956, in which the writer, Russell Annabel, tells of an Indian being carried off, presumably for dinner, by "Gilyuk, the shaggy cannibal giant sometimes called The-Big-Man-With-The-Little-Hat." The Indians knew that Gilyuk was around because they had seen his sign, a birch sapling about four inches through that had been twisted into shreds as a man might twist a match stick. The scene is set on the Nelchina Plateau, south of Tyone Lake [Alaska], sometime about the 1940s.[25]

Many things may snap or twist a tree, of course. Bigfoot researchers focus chiefly on larger saplings, and on limbs above a normal bear's or human's reach, where no other apparent cause of damage is apparent. John Christman once observed a line of broken saplings standing parallel to Bigfoot tracks on Washington State's Olympic Peninsula. Dr. Wolf-Henrich Fahrenbach refers specifically to breakage of green limbs, two or three inches thick, where "damage does indeed appear to be related to the twisting by an animal with superhuman strength combined with a powerful and flexible grip which twists the stem, splintering it internally, without shredding or removing the bark."[26]

Bigfoot "nests" are something else, entirely. Various prosimians and great apes habitually build nests for sleeping and, in some species, for raising offspring. Around age three, gorillas start constructing ground nests two to five feet in diameter, initially in close proximity to their mothers. Bonobos, chimpanzees, and orangutans normally build their nests in trees. If Bigfoot exists, we should expect similar nesting behavior, but Dr. John Bindernagel blames it on

---

Photo of a typical "tree twist" sometimes attributed to Bigfoot. Credit: Author's collection.

"functionally inappropriate" behavior, caused by stress from habitat loss, contact with humans, or other adverse factors.[27] Ohio's Bigfoot takes its "Grassman" nickname from heaps of dry grass it allegedly piles into domes, but many photos of purported Bigfoot nests clearly owe much to wishful thinking on the part of the photographers.

Worldwide, BHMs have long been blamed for stealing, devouring, or simply mutilating various animals, ranging in size from rodents, cats, and dogs to livestock such as calves, hogs, and Tibetan yaks. Pursuit of deer has been reported frequently, some hunters claiming that their kills were snatched by Bigfoot. Ohio researchers link BHMs to unexplained deer kills, including cases where the legs were broken, sometimes with the carcass disemboweled but otherwise untouched. Matt Moneymaker found his first "deer kill stash" in November 1992 while investigating a rash of sightings in eastern Ohio, and has been collecting data ever since. He theorizes that BHMs kill deer for their livers, which contain "substantial amounts of every vitamin necessary for life, particularly those which would become naturally depleted during the fall and winter."[28]

We have many diverse reports of BHMs damaging property, usually by accident, less often through aggressive action. According to the stories, they have raided sheds and porches, stolen food from outdoor freezers, broken fences, dented roadside signs—and, if we believe John Reed, founder of Pennsylvania's Lykens Valley Sasquatch Hunters, vandalized Reed's Winnebago motor home in October 2012, first shattering an outdoor light to mask the crime. Police blamed the damage on humans, while Reed called it "a warning from Sasquatch to get off his territory."[29]

On January 11, 2014, Anthony Pailla called police in Breckenridge, Michigan, to report an ongoing campaign of harassment by Bigfoot. Deputy Thomas Anderson's report explains that "Anthony believes Bigfoot is not [an] ape man or a mammal at all, but a spiritual creature that can shape shift, but when it takes form eats pizza and defecates." Pailla surmised that he woke "the spirit of Bigfoot" in 1997 by "knocking branches against trees to break them into smaller pieces," and thus attracted its unwelcome attention. Since then, the beast had plagued him, vandalizing his home, stealing numerous pizzas, and leaving heaps of scat behind. As proof, Pailla presented officers with boxes full of excrement.[30]

Deputy Anderson wrote: "He was kindly told that DNA processing is only used for serious crimes and that Bigfoot is not a suspect in any criminal activity. I explained that scat would not contain DNA, and he was reminded that MSP [Michigan State Police] won't process it."[31]

So far, purported "Bigfoot nests" have yielded
no hard evidence of occupation by unknown primates.
Credit: Author's collection.

Primates vocalize for many reasons. Humankind is not unique in making sounds, whether they be alarms or laughter, snarls of anger, mating calls, or the "pant-hoot" cries of chimpanzees, regarded by some primatologists as a form of dialect. Bigfoot, in turn, has been described as whistling, grunting, howling, roaring, "tooth popping," and shrieking like an actress in a horror film. Theodore Roosevelt, in his tale of trapper Bauman (Chapter 1), writes of the killer beast that "several times it uttered a harsh, grating, long-drawn moan, a peculiarly sinister sound."[32]

The first known person to record purported Bigfoot vocalizations was Alan Berry, a mining geologist and Vietnam War veteran who taped the sounds on October 21, 1972, while camped with friends in California's Sierra Nevada Mountains. Analysis of Berry's recording suggested that the author of those sounds possessed a vocal tract 9.8 inches long. The vocal tract of a six-foot-tall man, by contrast, measures around 6.6 inches—suggesting that the howler Berry taped would stand no less than seven and one-half feet tall.[33]

That estimate, predictably, sparked controversy. Dr. Grover Krantz, despite his personal belief in Bigfoot's existence, stood with the nay-sayers, writing that he had "listened to at least ten such tapes and find no compelling reason to believe that any of them are what the recorders claimed them to be." With specific regard to Berry's recording, Krantz wrote, "One…tape was analyzed by some university sound specialists who determined that a human voice could not have made them; they required a much longer vocal tract. A Sasquatch investigator later asked one of these experts if a human could imitate the sound characteristics by simply cupping his hands around his mouth. The answer was yes."[34]

Today, dozens of "Bigfoot calls" are readily available for listening online, from Berry's premiere tape to recent recordings on YouTube. At least three websites are devoted to purported Sasquatch sounds (see Chapter 8), and monster hunters with money to burn may purchase an "Official Bigfoot Call," hand-carved, with a lanyard attached for easy carrying in the deep woods, for just $64.90.[35]

Hair Today, Gone Tomorrow

Countless hairs have been collected over decades, at or near the scenes of Bigfoot sightings. Many prove to be from well-known species—humans, wildlife, or domestic animals—but some have yielded curious results under analysis.

Entrepreneurs cash in on the search for Bigfoot hair samples. Credit: Author's collection.

The first sample to undergo such testing was collected by Ivan Sanderson at Bluff Creek, California, in 1958. Dr. F. Martin Duncan, head of the London Zoo's extensive animal hair collection, examined the strands, reporting that they "did not match any known North American mammal, but that they would be from an unknown and very large primate."[36]

In 1993, Dr. Sterling Bunnell, a member of the California Academy of Sciences, studied hair samples collected at Damnation Creek, in northern California, and reported:

I have examined the hair specimen...and compared it by light microscopy under direct and transmitted illumination with human, chimpanzee, gorilla, orangutan, and Pygathrix [douc langur] monkey hair. It is clearly related to the human-chimpanzee-gorilla group, but is distinguishable from each of these. On the basis of surface and internal structure it seems more like gorilla hair than human or chimp, while by the same criteria human and chimp appear closely related. The specimen hairs are remarkable in the extremely fine and diffuse pigmentation (the other species show dark melanin clumps and medullary streaks) and the absence of observable medullary structure.[37]

On August 5, 1995, researchers Paul Freeman, Bill Laughery and Wes Sumerlin followed three sets of footprints and a trail of twisted saplings through the Blue Mountains east of Walla Walla, Washington, collecting two separate sets of hair samples en route, before sighting a Bigfoot through binoculars. Dr. Wolf-Henrich Fahrenbach examined the hairs microscopically, pronouncing them samples from two members of the same species, different in length and color, "indistinguishable from human hair by any criterion."[38]

After a nationwide search of DNA laboratories, Fahrenbach chose Dr. Paul Fuerst at Ohio State University's Department of Molecular Genetics to examine the samples, with graduate student J. A. Poe. In January 1998, Fahrenbach announced near completion of an article on the hair samples, planned for submission to the International Society of Cryptozoology's annual peer-reviewed journal. Sadly, financial difficulties forced the ISC to disband that same year, and Fahrenbach amended his statement in March, writing:

After lengthy deliberation, we...have decided to withhold submission of the manuscript of the analysis until more DNA from tissue, preferably with attached hair, is obtained. Our studies have not yielded a sequenced mitochondrial gene fragment to determine the phylogenetic affiliation of the creature. The ambiguous results at the present time can, on the one hand, generate misplaced enthusiasm and be quoted as "proof," or on the other hand, can be used by the opposite camp to criticize and denigrate the results unfairly. This decision emphasizes the critical need to obtain tissue samples rather than hair alone. Such should be fresh blood or possibly minimal shreds of torn skin caught on some obstruction. Feces are not suitable at the present time.[39]

Speaking of feces, multiple mounds of purported Bigfoot scat have been collected since 1968, when Ivan Sanderson described a sample shipped to Dr. William Charles Osman Hill, a British primatologist and anatomist then employed by the London Zoological Society. Sanderson's summary of Hill's findings was tantalizing.

I wish we had space to give you their report in full. It is quite amazing. The points of significance in it are as follows: In general, this fecal mass did not in any way resemble that of any known North American animal. On the other hand, it did look humanoid, but it had some peculiar features, as if the lower bowel had a spiral twist. But above all, it was composed exclusively of vegetable matter and this as far as could be identified of local California fresh water plants. The real clincher, however was that it contained the eggs and desiccated remains of certain larvae otherwise known only in (a) some North American Indian tribal groups in the Northwest, (b) pigs imported from south China, (c) human beings in country districts in southwest China and (d) in pigs in that same area.[40]

Eight years earlier, Robert Titmus had gathered alleged Bigfoot hair and scat while on retainer with Tom Slick's search team, but both samples proved to come from moose—a major problem, since that species is unknown in California and Oregon. That discovery has led some critics to accuse Titmus of fraud, and author Joshua Blu Buhs goes further, suggesting that John Green, a close friend of Titmus, may have helped aided in the hoax.[41]

Peter Byrne, another Slick team member, also viewed Titmus as a hoaxer, claiming some of the "Bigfoot scat" he collected came from a Yurok Indian's pony. Following that episode, Byrne wrote that Slick "was not about to have anything to do with [Titmus] after what we all laughingly called 'The Great Pony Poop Caper.' Nor was I nor any of my associates."[42]

For what it may be worth, a bitter feud endures between Byrne and John Green to the present day, with Green repeatedly calling Byrne a fraud.[43] In 2005, Green refused to supply a photo to illustrate his entry in my *Encyclopedia of Cryptozoology* unless I promised to expunge Byrne's name from the 3,200-page manuscript. In December 2013, Green widely posted news of Byrne's sentencing on charges of Social Security fraud.

Another case involving alleged BHM hair surfaced in August 2008, when Josh Gates and his team from television's *Destination Truth* (see Chapter 8) found supposed Yeti hair in India. British primatologist Ian Redmond told London's *Daily Mail* that the hairs "are the most positive evidence yet that a yeti might possibly exist."[44] By then, Redmond had ruled out black bears, macaque monkeys, dogs and wild boar as contributors of the hair samples. Bigfooters' hopes were dashed two months later, when the hairs were identified as coming from a Himalayan goat. Undaunted, Gates and company tried again in 2009, this time in Bhutan, finding more hairs that Gates delivered to DNA Diagnostics Inc. in Timpson, Texas. There, Dr. Melba Ketchum—described in differing accounts as a simple veterinarian and a forensic analyst with "impressive credentials"—pronounced the hairs those of a "very large primate" whose DNA sequence "did not match any of those that are in the animal species worldwide DNA database."[45]

The same anonymous blogger who posted that news describes DNA Diagnostics as "world renowned for myriad methods of DNA testing, both animal and human."[46] A search online revealed that the lab—founded in 1985—had no active website in March 2014, but it did rate mention on the Better Business Bureau's website, where it holds a grade of "F." Reasons listed for the failing grade include seven complaints from customers spanning a three-year period, with five unresolved. Three complaints dealt with "delivery issues," while four involved "problems with products/services." Also noted was the lab's "failure to respond to one complaint filed against [the] business."[47]

Proof Positive?

DNA may be the only tool available to prove Bigfoot's existence without delivery of a corpse or captive specimen. Sadly, so far it has proved to be, at best, a titillating dead end. First reported in 1986 by Sir Alec Jeffreys at England's University of Leicester, DNA profiling made its American court debut one year later, convicting Florida rapist Tommie Lee Andrews. Since then, DNA labs and data banks have blanketed the country, jailing thousands of felons, exonerating many wrongfully convicted prisoners, and settling countless paternity cases.

But can DNA prove Bigfoot's existence? The case of "Zana" is instructive.

In the latter nineteenth century, villagers from Tkhina, in the Ochimchiri District of Abkhazia, Western Caucasus, captured a "wild woman" whom they called Zana, believed to be a female specimen of Russia's *abnauayu* "abominable snowman." Zana eventually became "tame," and mated with—or was raped by—various male villagers, producing several children. At her death, she was buried in an unmarked grave outside Tkhina, while some of her children lived on. The last to die, in 1954, was a son named Khwit. After three failed attempts to find Zana's grave in the 1970s, Russian researcher Dmitri Bayanov exhumed Khwit and took his skull to Moscow, for examination by two physical anthropologists. Their 1987 report, pre DNA, states that:

The Tkhina skull exhibits an original combination of modern and ancient features.... The facial section of the skull is significantly larger in comparison with the mean Abkhaz type...All the measurements and indices of the superciliary cranial contour are greater not only than those of the mean Abkhaz series, but also than those of maximum size of some fossil skulls studied (or rather were comparable with the latter). The Tkhina skull approaches closest the Neolithic Vovnigi II skulls of the fossil series....The skull discloses a great deal of peculiarity, a certain disharmony disequilibrium in its features, very large dimensions of the facial skeleton, increased development of the contour of the skull, specificity of the non-metric features (the two foramina mentale in the lower jaw, the intrusive bones in the sagittal suture, and the Inca bone). The skull merits further extended study.[48]

DNA solved the mystery in 2013, when Dr. Bryan Sykes, professor of human genetics at the University of Oxford, examined one of Khwit's teeth, determining that his mother had been "genetically 100 percent sub-Saharan African"—not an *abnauayu* at all, but a misplaced visitor from the Dark Continent.[49] We shall never know how she arrived in Abkhazia, eventually becoming a captive sex slave.

Other cases remain ambiguous. In June 2001, *The Times* of London published results of DNA analysis on supposed Yeti hair collected in Bhutan. Led by an "official Yeti-hunter," zoologist Dr. Rob McCall had retrieved the sample from a tree. Back at Oxford, Dr. Sykes tested the hair, reporting, "We found some DNA in it, but we don't know what it is. It's not a human, not a bear nor anything else we have so far been able to identify. It's a mystery and I never thought this would end in a mystery. We have never encountered DNA that we couldn't recognize before."[50]

Eleven years later, in May 2012, Dr. Sykes broadcast a call for any and all available Bigfoot or Yeti hair samples, declaring, "I'm challenging and inviting the cryptozoologists to come up with the evidence instead of complaining that science is rejecting what they have to say. As an academic I have certain reservations about entering this field, but I think using genetic analysis is entirely objective; it can't be falsified. So I don't have to put myself into the position of either believing or disbelieving these creatures."[51]

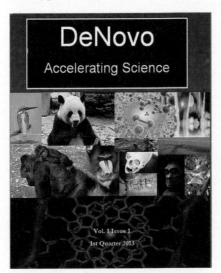

DeNovo's first—and so far, only—issue, presenting a controversial report on supposed Bigfoot DNA. Credit: Author's collection.

Meanwhile, in the States, exciting things seemed to be happening. Hair samples bagged by Cliff Barackman in Oklahoma while taping an episode of TV's *Finding Bigfoot* (see Chapter 8) went to DNA Solutions in Oklahoma City, but Dr. Brandt Cassidy was unable to extract any testable genetic material. Microscopic examination revealed that "[w]hile superficially similar to a person's hair, the hair did not appear to be human in origin. First off the hair shafts had tapered ends which would indicate that the hairs had never been subjected to a hair cut. Another difference that was found was that the medulla width was different than what is commonly found among humans."[52]

The bomb dropped three months later, on February 13, 2013, when an article in the *DeNovo Journal of Science* announced that the Sasquatch Genome Project (SGP)—a self-described "collaboration by an interdisciplinary team of scientists from independent, public, and academic laboratories, aided by volunteer researchers and supporters, who seek to understand the nature of the indigenous, aboriginal people in North America commonly known as Bigfoot or Sasquatch, primarily through the study of their DNA"[53]—had evidence in hand proving that Bigfoot is a kind of human hybrid.

The abstract of that article deserves quotation here. Readers interested in the full report may purchase copies on *DeNovo*'s website, at http://denovojournal.com/denovo_002.htm.

One hundred eleven samples of blood, tissue, hair, and other types of specimens were studied, characterized and hypothesized to be obtained from elusive hominins in North America commonly referred to as Sasquatch. DNA was extracted and purified from a subset of these samples that survived rigorous screening for wildlife species identification. Mitochondrial DNA (mtDNA) sequencing, specific genetic loci sequencing, forensic short tandem repeat (STR) testing, whole genome single nucleotide polymorphism (SNP) bead array analysis, and next generation whole genome sequencing were conducted on purported Sasquatch DNA samples gathered from various locations in North America. Additionally, histopathologic and electron microscopic examination were performed on a large tissue sample. The mtDNA whole genome haplotypes obtained were uniformly consistent with modern humans. Of the 20 whole and 10 partial mitochondrial genomes sequenced, 16 diverse haplotypes were found suggesting that these hominins did not originate in a single geographic location. In contrast, consistent, reproducible, novel data were obtained when nuclear DNA was amplified utilizing various platforms. Nuclear DNA obtained from Sasquatch samples produced novel SNPs, off ladder alleles on human STRs, retained human sequence interspersed with novel sequence, and whole genome SNPs that fell outside the human threshold. Three of the Sasquatch samples were subjected to next generation whole genome sequencing, each of which independently yielded high quality complete genomes. Analysis of preliminary phylogeny trees derived from supercontigs generated from all three samples showed homology to human chromosome 11 reference sequence hg 19, and to primate sequences. The totality of the DNA evidence suggests the Sasquatch nuclear DNA is a mosaic comprising human DNA interspersed with sequence that is novel but primate in origin. In summary, our data indicates that the Sasquatch has human mitochondrial DNA but possesses nuclear DNA that is a structural mosaic consisting of human and novel non-human DNA.[54]

The reaction was immediate, predictably split along preconceived fault lines of doubt and belief. Skeptics panned the study as hokum, while devoted Bigfoot hunters quarreled among themselves, accepting or rejecting the announcement. The BFRO's Matt Moneymaker cautiously endorsed the report, saying, "I do believe a wheel has been set in motion that was not in motion before."[55] David Paulides, of North American Bigfoot Research, was a more ardent supporter— in fact, claiming credit for initiating the study, and for furnishing a majority of the DNA samples examined.[56] Researcher Tim Fasano branded Paulides a liar, Paulides responded in kind, and so it goes throughout the "Bigfoot community."[57]

Authors of the article, immediately under fire, include:

- Dr. Melba Ketchum, a veterinarian who completed her doctoral studies at Texas A&M University and founded DNA Diagnostics in 1985 while a visiting scientist at the University of Kentucky's Animal Genetic Testing and Research Laboratory. The SGP's website calls her a member and former treasurer of the Association of Forensic DNA Analysts and Administrators, further noting that she "has chaired or served on a number of international committees and projects through the International Society for Animal Genetics."[58]
- Dr. Patrick Wojkiewicz, employed at the Shreveport Laboratory of the North Louisiana Crime Lab System since 1977, presently serving as its director and technical leader of the DNA section, as well as an adjunct assistant professor of chemistry at Northwestern State University of Louisiana.[59]
- Aliece Watts, president of Integrated Forensic Laboratories Inc., in Euless, Texas. In 2009 she was one of three scientists removed from the Texas Forensic Science Commission by Governor Rick Perry, after they criticized evidence used to convict and execute supposed killer arsonist Cameron Todd Willingham.60
- David W. Spence, trace evidence supervisor with the Southwestern Institute of Forensic Sciences Criminal Investigations Laboratory in Dallas, and a past participant in FBI forensic science symposiums.[61]
- Dr. Andreas Holzenburg, a German transplant who earned his Ph.D. from the University of Göttingen, now serving as director of the Microscopy & Imaging Center at Texas A&M University.[62]
- Dr. Douglas G. Toler, a clinical pathologist at Huguley Memorial Hospital in Fort Worth for thirty years, now chief of Huguley Pathology Consultants in Burleson, Texas.[63]
- Dr. Tom Prychitko, a molecular biologist who earned his master's and doctorate degrees from Detroit's Wayne State University, and an adjunct instructor for his alma mater's Biology Department, said to be "a firm believer that science has no boundaries."[64]

Hardly a group of kooks from the fringe, yet the SGP team met ardent—sometimes vitriolic—opposition from skeptics and certain Bigfoot researchers alike. One bone of contention was the *DeNovo Journal of Science*, apparently created specifically to publish the Bigfoot DNA study as a "special issue," with no other issues or articles released by the time *Seeking Bigfoot* went to press.[65] That, in turn, raised issues of legitimate peer review. Dr. Ketchum responded by saying:

We encountered the worst scientific bias in the peer review process in recent history. I am calling it the "Galileo Effect." Several journals wouldn't even read our manuscript when we sent them a pre-submission inquiry. Another one leaked our peer reviews. We were even mocked by one reviewer in his peer review. Rather than spend another five years just trying to find a journal to publish and hoping that decent, open minded reviewers would be chosen, we published [in *DeNovo*].[66]

Which, of course, is prima facie evidence to skeptics that no "legitimate" journal accepted the SGP's findings. True or false, the dead-end cycle of "convince us; we're not listening" is painfully familiar among the professional debunkers sometimes labeled "skofftics."

Complaints against the SGP study are summarized by an Internet blogger who calls him- or herself "idoubtit," writing for a website titled "Doubtful News." They include:

1. "There are PLENTY of journals that would have published this paper"—though "idoubtit" fails to name a single one.[67]
2. Judging the authors, he/she notes that "none are academics, but forensic specialists."[68] In fact, three of the authors—Doctors Holzenburg, Prychitko, and Wojkiewicz—hold university teaching positions, but is it even relevant, unless expertise hinges upon a prestigious academic position?
3. Publication in a new journal is "HIGHLY SUSPICIOUS."[69] Indeed, the article's only identified peer reviewer is David H. Swenson, Ph.D., described online as a biochemist with "over 39 journal publications to his credit."[70] Alas, the link to "his resume" leads to a website of advertisements for health insurance, job openings, and hairstyles, with no mention of Dr. Swenson.[71] In his brief online review, Swenson admits, "This collaborative venture has done a huge project that taxes me to fully grasp."[72]
4. *DeNovo's* special issue sells online for $30, thus allegedly preventing university reviewers from reading and critiquing it—an obstacle which has not frustrated "idoubtit's" condemnation, sight unseen. He/she writes, in conclusion, "As a good Skeptic [*sic*], I am COMPLETELY willing to change my mind if the paper itself provides scientific value. Based on what I've seen so far, I'm not hopeful."[73] Like the blogger's name, however, his/her qualifications to judge the work of multiple career forensic scientists remain unknown.

While that furor simmered in Texas and beyond, word came from Oxford University and Dr. Sykes, concerning his study of purported Bigfoot-Yeti DNA. In August 2013, Sykes wrote:

Thanks to all who have contributed samples to the project. We have collected and analyzed over thirty samples and results are being prepared for publication. Following normal procedure, no results or other information will be available prior to publication, so please do not enquire. Though the collection phase is now over, hair samples can still be submitted for analysis, but the costs (about $2,000 per sample) will no longer be covered.[74]

No date had been announced for publication of the university's findings when *Seeking Bigfoot* went to press, but ABC News broke a scoop on the story in October 2013. According to that report, the "small sample" on hand—"including a single hair found a decade ago, and the jawbone of a mummified animal discovered in the 1970s by a hunter"—suggests "that the animal many people have reported seeing may be an unknown species of bear, related to an extinct polar bear."[75] The report quotes Dr. Sykes as saying:

This is a species that hasn't been recorded for 40,000 years. Now, we know one of these was walking around ten years ago. And what's interesting is that we have found this type of animal at both ends of the Himalayas. If one were to go back, there would be others still there. The fact that the hunter, who had great experience of bears, thought this one was in some way unusual and was frightened of it, makes me wonder if this species of bear might behave differently. Maybe it is more aggressive, more dangerous or is more bipedal than other bears.[76]

No mention of North America's Bigfoot graced the report. And there, at least for now, the matter rests, in mystery.

CHAPTER 6

HOAXED!

Randy Lee Tenley played his last practical joke on Sunday night, August 26, 2012. Dressed in a ghillie suit, the forty-four-year-old prankster ran across US Highway 93 south of Kalispell, Montana, in the face of oncoming traffic. A fifteen-year-old driver struck him first, causing another car to swerve around the injured "Bigfoot," then a seventeen-year-old ran over Tenley, killing him. Montana Highway Patrol Lieutenant Colonel Butch Huseby told reporters, "This is one of the dumbest things I've ever seen."1

Indeed, and tragic for the joker's family. But it was not the first recorded Bigfoot hoax, and likely will not be the last.

One Born Every Minute

T he first known Bigfoot hoax—still taken seriously by some believers—began on July 4, 1884, when British Columbia's *Daily Colonist* reported the capture of a "British Columbia Gorilla." Reportedly stunned by a fall, the juvenile specimen, nicknamed "Jacko," was supposedly lodged in jail. Some 200 gawkers turned out to see it on July 10, but met only a jailer who vaguely fielded questions. Meanwhile, on July 9, the *Mainland Guardian* assured its readers "that no such animal was caught, and how the Colonist was duped in such a manner, and by such a story, is strange."

A poster for *The Legend of Bigfoot,* compiling hoaxed footage from Ivan Marx. Credit: Author's collection.

Over the next century, various hoaxers tried their hands at faking Bigfoot tracks (see Chapter 1), and produced various films allegedly depicting BHMs at large in the wild. In January 1976, longtime researcher Ivan Marx released his feature film *The Legend of Bigfoot*, including footage of actors clad in baggy costumes trudging through the woods. In one scene, narrated by Marx, "the shining eyes" of Bigfoot, visible across a lake, are clearly a car's headlights.

Predictably, some hoaxes have grown more sophisticated over time, with advances in technology. On November 14, 2005, one Mark Nelson, a self-described amateur naturalist and bass guitarist for a band called "Total Nutcase," posted the following message online:

Last weekend my girlfriend Jill and I were hiking in northern Sonoma County (in CA). We had our video camera with us so we could try to tape some elk. We'd been going for about a couple hours when Jill said she heard a strange noise. We stopped, and then I heard it too.

At first, it sounded like a deep growl, kind of what a bear would make, but higher pitched. Jill wanted to run away, but then we heard it again. I thought it was real strange. So I took out the camera to try to zoom in on where the noise was coming from, and there was this weird creature. It must have heard us, because it moved away real fast! It was gone in about fifteen seconds.

The thing was like eight to nine feet tall,

with reddish brown colored hair, and dark eyes. I ran after it, but it moved real fast. When I got to the spot in the ground where it had been when I first heard it, I noticed that the grass was smashed down, and there was this strange, skunky kind of smell.

Afterwards, Jill was real scared, so we turned around and went back, and we didn't see it again. But that creature was like nothing I've ever seen before—if it wasn't Bigfoot, then I don't know what it was.

And one more thing—when I got home, my Mom's mutt Brownie kept sniffing and barking at my hiking boots. They must have smelled like the creature. Brownie was going totally crazy. Luckily, my buddy Jeff has a buddy Alex who works in a lab, so we're going to have him analyze them. QUESTIONS? E-MAIL ME HERE OR CALL ME AT 805-264-7753.2

If it seemed odd for Nelson to have his own toll-free phone number, that was hardly the strangest part of the story. Word of "the Sonoma footage" spread like wildfire among Bigfoot researchers, but as they questioned Nelson, his story changed repeatedly. First, he could not decide if he lived in Oxnard or San Luis Obispo. Next, he denied any knowledge of Art Bell's radio program, though Nelson posted his tale to Bell's message board on November 16. The setting of his encounter switched from a "deer trail" to a "fire road," and no trace of his frightened girlfriend appeared in the footage. Mononymous buddies Jeff and Alex remained otherwise unidentified, as did Alex's mysterious "lab." Phone calls from researcher John Freitas were cut short when girlfriend Jill came home, "acting really jealous of the time I am taking on this video."[3]

While the BFRO's Matt Moneymaker seemed to accept the Nelson video as genuine, Thom Powell found the clip "suspicious, to put it mildly." Steve Kulls spoke more bluntly, saying the footage "reeks of a hoax," and William Dranginis agreed, calling it "a hoax, plain and simple." In fact, Dranginis went further, writing: "It is my opinion that the actions of the BFRO are nothing more than a novice attempt to generate national press coverage for their 'so-called' Bigfoot Expeditions. Why else would the 'Only Scientific Research Organization' do something like this?"[4]

The other shoe dropped in April 2006, when comedians Penn Jillette and Raymond Teller admitted sponsoring the hoax for their *Penn & Teller: Bullshit!* television series. In this case, the title says it all.

One of several Bigfoot suits available for purchase online and from costume shops. Credit: Author's collection.

An albino Yeti suit, for those who think the "Abominable Snowman" must be snowy white. Credit: Author's collection.

Baby Yarwen

Four months after Penn and Teller's revelation, on August 22, 2006, the Internet crackled with news of a "baby Bigfoot" sighting in Maine. On August 26, "Tuck Hayes" of New Jersey e-mailed a local BFRO member, asking: "Who do I contact to sell a Bigfoot body? I will have a complete body to sell soon. The bidding starts at $1,000,000 tax free. It will go to the highest bidder."[5] On September 1, a nominally different informant—"Dominick Perez"—claimed to have an infant BHM, whom he called "Yarwen," in custody. The creature was forty inches tall, weighed 121.5 pounds, and was docile despite its recent capture and transport to New Jersey. "I drove the thing all the way home," Perez wrote, "in the back of my truck handcuffed to the roll bar."[6]

Presumably, no other motorists observed it on the trip from Maine, across six states.

By September 2, when Loren Coleman entered the picture, "Perez" had admitted using a pseudonym—and he had boosted the price initially set by "Tuck Hayes." Now, Yarwen's captor demanded "$100,000 for photos which

Typical supermarket tabloid coverage of Bigfoot, complete with fake photographs. Credit: Author's collection.

you can come and take." Beyond that, he planned to "list the creature on eBay with an opening bid of $10,000,000." Coleman was welcome to "ten percent of whatever we eventually get, and you will have the honor of breaking the story." Based on their exchanges, Coleman (a former psychiatric social worker) diagnosed Perez as "psychologically erratic."[7]

From there, the tale began unraveling. On September 3, Perez promised a "live video" of Yarwen would be posted to eBay "in about a week." One day later, he offered the BFRO a hair sample for DNA testing, but insisted that "if you want to see this thing it will be done on MY terms. I risked my life to capture this thing not you. I cannot believe this. I would think that you would be jumping through hoops at the prospect of being able to validate your research. If a woman can sell a piece of grilled cheese in the image of the Virgin Mary for thousands, imagine what this is worth."[8]

September 6 brought another e-mail to the BFRO, reading:

I found one of you competitors who was wise enough to take me up on my generous offer. He has seen the creature (he actually fainted!), a ten- minute video has been made and you will see a huge announcement in the coming days. You blew it. I believe deep down you have no faith in your "research." You don't really believe they exist. You have seen countless disappointments and hoaxes and you have given up on believing. Now it has cost you millions and the legitimacy and recognition you so desperately seek. That honor has been granted to another. You losers profess to be cryptozoological investigators but you're naught but a bunch of frauds.[9]

The last e-mail from Perez reached Loren Coleman on September 9. It read:

Loren you fool!...You were given a once in a lifetime chance to see a live one (Bigfoot)? You passed up a killer offer... the...captured...bigfoot...sold...to a mystery bidder for 17 million. You could of had 1.7 mil! Anyway, the body of an adult (Bigfoot) is buried on the northermost banks of the royal river. Wanna go a diggin'?[10]

Coleman surmised that the episode might be another tawdry hoax "from you know who," but left the putative prankster unnamed.[11] As for Yarwen, the rest is silence.

The twenty-first century's most notorious Bigfoot hoax (so far) ostensibly began on June 10, 2008, with discovery of a BHM corpse in northern Georgia. As initially reported, the find was made by ex-prison guard Rick Dyer and police officer Matt Whitton while hunting, whereupon they summoned half a dozen friends to haul the carcass home and stash it in a freezer. Whitton posted his first YouTube clip announcing the discovery on July 9. Two weeks later, Dyer and Whitton staged a press conference in Jonesboro, Georgia, and the ripples spread. On July 28 the pair told their story on "Squatchdetective Radio," inviting host Steve Kulls and researcher Tom Biscardi to view the remains. Biscardi, we're told, flew to Georgia on August 1 to collect DNA.[12]

A word about the new arrival on the scene must be inserted here. Born in 1948, Carmine Thomas Biscardi became fascinated with Bigfoot after viewing Roger Patterson's footage in 1967. Four years later, he created Amazing Horizons Inc. to distribute films from Ivan Marx, now universally viewed as hoaxes. *Saga* magazine ran a feature article on Biscardi and then-partner Gene Findley in December 1973, quoting the hunters on their commitment to capturing Bigfoot

A 1983 press release, including hoaxed photos, circulated to promote a film by Tom Biscardi. Credit: Author's collection.

Bigfoot photos amaze experts

By DICK DONOVAN

An amazing series of pictures that captured a Bigfoot bathing in a mountain stream is the first conclusive proof that the legendary creature of the wilds really lives!

The photographs, which clearly show the massive beast, were made from the frames of a two-minute, 28-second film shot near Snow Mountain in Northern California. The astonishing photos are the result of years of searching by a daring and determined crew of Bigfoot hunters from Amazing Horizons Inc., based in San Jose, Calif.

"The expedition team from Amazing Horizons had been on the trail of Bigfoot for years before the film was made," C. Thomas Biscardi, president of the group, told The NEWS in an exclusive interview.

"We have reports on sightings coming in from all over the nation and we've searched extensively throughout the seven main states where the beast has been seen most often. Finally, our efforts paid off. We got the most astounding film footage of Bigfoot ever made."

out to investigate the sighting.

"After searching the area for some time, we sighted the beast and our photographer started his camera rolling. It was ankle-deep in water about 100 to 150 yards away.

"Even from where we were we could see that the creature was over 8 feet tall and weighed a minimum of 500 pounds. It had reddish hair and was splashing water over its body probably to rid itself of mosquitoes, flies and bugs."

Biscardi said the Bigfoot is a fully grown adult male, and he believes it to be the same creature often sighted in the area in recent years.

Photographs made from the film were shown to anthropologist-historian Dr. Warren Cook, at Castleton State College in Vermont for authenti

The monster emerges from brush (top)

in Alaska. "Hell, somebody's got to do it," Biscardi said. "I've sunk so much money in this thing now—so has Gene—that I have bad dreams at night. There's this huge bill collector dressed up in a Bigfoot suit." Still, it wasn't all hardship, as *Saga* reporter William Childress noted, interviewing Biscardi "in his luxurious San Jose, Calif., apartment, waiting for the latest word on any sightings from Ivan Marx and the other six members of the Alaskan expedition."[13]

Ten years later, with no monster in hand, Biscardi produced and distributed *In the Shadow of Bigfoot*, a feature film chock-full of more Marx footage. Biscardi then dropped off the Bigfoot radar until January 2004, when he resurfaced to solicit $1 million in corporate donations to finance a new expedition. As detailed in Biscardi's press release, "The timing of this current expedition was prompted by the recent sighting and news reports of an 'albino' Bigfoot. Biscardi has seen and has a photo of a baby Bigfoot with white fur…The photo was taken by tracker, Peggy Marx [Ivan's wife]."[14]

That scheme fizzled, but Biscardi rebounded on April 19, 2005, claiming a personal Bigfoot sighting—while accompanied by Ivan Marx's grandchildren—near Burney, California. They were close enough to bag the beast but, alas, Biscardi had "left his tranquilizer gun and his wire-mesh grenade launcher at home." A new press release, issued on June 29, declared "Imminent Capture Anticipated," referring interested parties to Biscardi's public relations firm. Days later, he established a website live-streaming coverage of an expedition to the Klamath River Valley, viewable by subscription for $19.95 per week. The goal: to tranquilize Bigfoot for medical examination, then release it back into the wild. August 19 brought Biscardi's announcement that "we have a Bigfoot," specifically an eight-foot tall, 400-pound male, judged by some unknown means to be seventeen years old. That bubble burst on August 23 with Biscardi's admission that he had been "hoodwinked" by unnamed hoaxers.[15]

Apparently unfazed by bad publicity, Biscardi returned in June 2006, claiming to possess a "Bigfoot hand" found by some anonymous Montana policeman. X-rays identified the moldering relic as a black bear's severed paw. One month later, Biscardi sued the Great American Bigfoot Research Organization for allegedly cheating him out of $185,000 in salary and Biscardi's own archives, loaned to the outfit but never returned. Two of the GABRO's directors were Jimmy and Lee Hickman, grandsons of Ivan Marx. The outcome of that lawsuit is unknown, but 2007 found Biscardi back in action as the chief of Searching for Bigfoot, a group self-described on its website as "legendary."[16]

Flash forward to August 2, 2008, when Biscardi phoned Steve Kulls saying he (Biscardi) was "right there when the DNA was cut from the body" in Georgia, adding, "This thing has incredibly thick skin." Biscardi called again on August 9, announcing plans to measure and photograph the corpse. A third call, one day later, vouched for the body's authenticity, describing its eyes, teeth, genitals, and feet. Rumors circulated of a Bigfoot autopsy film, offered for sale with an $11 million price tag. August 11 saw the Georgia creature's first photo leaked to YouTube. Loren Coleman reportedly traced the "leak" back to Biscardi.[17]

The strange case took another jarring, mercenary turn on August 14, when

Indiana resident William Wald Lett Jr. announced that he had purchased the frozen corpse from Dyer and Whitton, driving it back to his Hoosier home. The next day, Biscardi joined Dyer and Whitton for a press conference in California, announcing that Dr. Curt Nelson, a molecular biologist at the University of Minnesota, had identified their "Bigfoot" sample as a mixture of human and opossum DNA. Biscardi rebutted that finding by claiming "the tissue sample was from the intestine of the animal, and that the animal had eaten an opossum"—a suggestion Dr. Nelson deemed "improbable."[18]

While Biscardi and company held court in California, Steve Kulls landed in Indiana, viewing the corpse in its block of ice. Laborious thawing began, revealing a rubber foot and artificial hair by August 16. Dyer and Whitton confessed their hoax to journalists on August 18, resulting in Whitton's dismissal from the Clayton County Police Department one day later. On August 20, the pair blamed Biscardi and Kulls for "coaching" them through the hoax. Kulls formally denied involvement, appearing on TV's *Fox and Friends* the next morning, to lambaste "the deceptions of Tom Biscardi."[19]

The end of yet another tawdry hoax? Alas, not quite.

Apparently convinced that time erases memory, Rick Dyer surfaced yet again in December 2012 with claims of having another Bigfoot in his freezer. Dyer had not stumbled over this one accidentally, but rather had shot it dead near San Antonio, Texas, with a BBC film crew watching, while the creature nibbled meat set out as bait. After disarming Dyer, the crew measured his kill at seven feet eight inches tall, tipping some convenient scale at 480 pounds. A few days after the shooting, Dyer's companions allegedly discarded him, claiming all rights to the footage for "Minnow Films," described on its current website as "an award-winning independent production company, renowned for its sensitive and intelligent portrayal of powerful human stories."[20] The finished product, Minnow spokesmen said, would air at New York's Tribeca Film Festival in April 2013.

That deadline passed without a glimpse of any footage—or a Bigfoot body—but Minnow Films still advertises *Shooting Bigfoot* as a feature "coming soon." Tom Biscardi dominates the trailer shown online, declaring, "This may be my last expedition. And this may be the time, once and for all, when we're going to solve this thing."[21]

Rick Dyer, meanwhile, refused to be forgotten. On August 2, 2013—the fifth anniversary of Tom Biscardi's claim that he had witnessed flesh carved from the nonexistent Georgia BHM—Dyer announced (through an intermediary) that "not only was there a Bigfoot shot and killed in San Antonio, Texas, on September 6, 2012, but when the Bigfoot was shot, there was a baby Bigfoot that was nearby which was gentle and Rick Dyer was able to pick it up in his arms. When the dead Bigfoot was taken for study and X-rayed, it was found to have both male and female organs and had a dead fetus inside one of it's two stomachs. So, there are two dead Bigfoot's [*sic*], not just one."[22]

Plus the living "baby," of course—or, maybe not.

No further news about the captive infant had been published by September 2013, when the following advertisement appeared online (shown here uncorrected):

An advertisement for Rick Dyer's video detailing his alleged slaying of two Bigfoot creatures.
Credit: Author's collection.

"After The Shot"
Pre-Order it NOW!

Time is running out. This is the most amazing footage ever filmed.

In case you have not been watching the Rick Dyer & Team Tracker Show on YouTube each nite, here is some bonus offers that come along with each purchase of this historic DVD called "After the Shot."

Each person who purchased this DVD will be invited to our special party in December in Las Vegas where you will also get to view the Bigfoot body. That's right, you read that correctly. You will get to see the Bigfoot body at this event. This is your chance to see this remarkable being that Rick Dyer shot and killed on September 6, 2012, in San Antonio, Texas.

That is well worth the $129.00 pre-order price. If you have been waiting to buy the DVD that shows what happened after the shot was fired. DON'T WAIT any longer. Get yours now before the price goes up to $200.00

The time has finally come. Bigfoot is indeed real and has been confirmed as an unknown being to science. The world is going to change as you and I currently know it. There is going to be a Bigfoot media frenzy all over the entire world and you have a chance to see if before the rest of the world does. Don't let this chance of a lifetime slip away. Order this DVD today, don't wait any longer. This DVD will never be offered again. Only 100 copies will ever be sold, so reserve your now. You won't want to miss this opportunity to have this disc in your home to show your family, friends and neighbors. The holiday giving season is almost here, This is going to be a Bigfoot Christmas staring with the Team Tracker party and the first viewing of "Hank" the Bigfoot body.[23]

Predictably, there was no revelation in Las Vegas. Instead, Dyer hired promoter Andrew Clacy to arrange an "I Told You So" tour featuring—you guessed it—the dead Texas Bigfoot on ice. Clacy told reporters "the body has undergone DNA testing, MRI scans, an autopsy, and more scientific testing in the last year. However, results from those tests are not yet available." The tour's first stop, in Phoenix, Arizona, was canceled when Clacy and Dyer could not find a venue. Next, they tried the International UFO Congress in Scottsdale, but were quickly rebuffed. That event's organizer, Maureen Elsberry, told journalists, "He's a known hoaxer. We are a reputable conference and we did not want to be associated with that."[24]

Dr. Michael Shermer, executive director of the Skeptics Society, was equally blunt. "Science is not done by promotional tours," he told CBS 5 News in Phoenix. "Why hasn't he submitted the body for scientists to analyze? The answer is obvious: it's a fake. If he has nothing to hide then let him show it to the professionals first before taking his victory lap."[25]

Do not expect Dyer and company to disappear. Nor should you hold your breath awaiting any glimpse of "Hank."

CHAPTER 7

THE WEIRD WORLD WEB

You may have difficulty spotting Bigfoot in the wild, but no shortage of groups devoted to the quest is found in cyberspace. This chapter reviews pertinent websites, Facebook pages, and newsgroups devoted to research and debate surrounding BHMs. I've attempted to make these selections as complete as possible, but I should warn readers if they are blindly searching online, some still "live" are long out of date. That said, some of the outdated ones do have info not found elsewhere, All links were "live" at press time, but given the Internet's fluidity, that may change at any moment. Except where quoted directly from others, the views expressed are mine alone.

N o self-respecting Bigfoot hunter(s) would be caught dead in the modern world without a Web page to announce their latest efforts and, where possible, make a profit from the effort. Sites are listed alphabetically below, with brief commentary reflecting this author's observations.

▶ **Alabama Bigfoot Society**
http://alabamabigfootsociety.com.
Founder Jim Smith leads this no-kill group "dedicated to the research and preservation of this creature and its habitat." The site includes reports of recent sightings, as well as information on black panther reports from the Cotton State and a haunted house in Dadeville.

▶ **Alabama-Georgia Research Group**
http://ag-bigfoot-research.tripod.com.
Founded by husband-wife researchers Anthony and April Yawn, after Anthony experienced two personal Bigfoot sightings, the AGRG exists "to gather positive proof that the creature, Bigfoot, exists." Their site includes photo galleries of tracks and expeditions, several sighting reports, and a $15 DVD examining the group's research techniques.

▶ **Allegheny Bigfoot Research Group**
http://alleghenybigfootresearchgroup.webs.com.
Based in Pennsylvania, this small group claims seven members, all but one identified by pseudonyms. Site owner "Anthony" bills himself as the ABRG's only fulltime researcher. The page includes a gallery of photos last updated in January 2012.

▶ **Alliance of Independent Bigfoot Researchers**
www.bigfootresearch.com
Chaired by Tom Yamarone, the AIBR offers an online archive of relevant articles dating from September 2005, plus active links to various other websites.

▶ **Arizona Bigfoot Center**
http://members.tripod.com/arizona_bigfoot/main.htm
Director Lyle Vann, writing in third-person, reports that he "often sees the creature when he goes hiking the rugged desert country of central and northern Arizona. He says the animals are reclusive and shy creatures—nocturnal for the most part—and expert at camouflaging themselves." The site includes Vann's own purported Bigfoot photos, plus information on Arizona UFO sightings.

▶ Arizona Cryptozoological Research Organization

http://azcro.lefora.com.

This page is a "members forum and blogosphere," rather than a website per se. Contributions are invited.

▶ Arkansas Bigfoot Tracker

http://arkansasbigfoottracker.weebly.com/index.html

Sparse at first glance, the ABT site offers a list of Arkansas Bigfoot reports, including both originals and others borrowed from the Gulf Coast Bigfoot Research Organization's website.

▶ Australian Ape Project

http://theaustralianapeproject.blogspot.com

BHMs are seen on every inhabited continent, and this site surveys the subject Down Under, billing itself as "the official Australian Ape page." Founded and led by Ray Doherty, the group has been active online since 2012, collecting some intriguing photographs.

▶ Australian Yowie Research

www.yowiehunters.com.au

Dean Harrison's website, launched in 1997—five years before the "official" site just mentioned—offers extensive information on the search for Bigfoot's Australian cousin, known on the island continent as "Yowie." Sightings recorded from Australia's various states are supplemented by historical articles dating from the 19th century and discussion of other cryptids, including mystery cats, relict thylacines, and "bunyips." Well worth visiting.

▶ The Beast of Boggy Creek

www.foukemonster.net

Devoted to the Arkansas BHM reported from Fouke and environs for over a century, this site includes a list of sightings from 1908 onward, a photo gallery, and various items of merchandise for sale.

A "Bigfoot Crossing" sign on one of California's rural highways, putting a humorous twist on repeated sightings. Credit: Author's collection.

▶ Bigfoot Ballyhoo

http://bigfootballyhoo.blogspot.com

Operated since October 2009 by husband-wife researchers Christopher Perry and Linda Newton-Perry, Bigfoot Ballyhoo draws occasional fire from critics for its wait-and-see attitude toward hoaxer Rick Dyer and alleged support of other apparently fraudulent claims (see Chapter 4).

► Bigfoot Encounters

www.bigfootencounters.com

Launched by late researcher Bobbie Short in 1995, this website has thankfully survived her passing in May 2013. It is a priceless resource including an archive with hundreds of magazine and newspaper articles; an interactive map listing Bigfoot sightings by state and Canadian province; photos, video and audio clips; scientific papers; interviews; book reviews; and a great deal more.

► Bigfoot Evidence

http://bigfootevidence.blogspot.com

Billed as the "World's Only 24/7 Bigfoot News Blog," Bigfoot Evidence presents many photos, video clips, and purported eyewitness accounts for what they may be worth, "encouraging readers to draw their own conclusions from the evidence and arguments."

► Bigfoot Field Journal

http://bf-field-journal.blogspot.com

A supporter of the controversial Ketchum DNA study (see Chapter 6), site owner Scott Carpenter dates his interest in BHMs from 1972–73, when "two juvenile hairy bipeds" visited his rural home. His site includes audio clips, sighting reports, and photos of "gifts" allegedly left at his home by Bigfoot: feathers, a hawk's skull, stacked stones, and so on.

► Bigfoot Field Reporter

http://bigfootlives.blogspot.com

When visited in March 2014, this page consisted of links to other websites.

► Bigfoot in Mississippi

www.bigfoot_in_mississippi.webs.com

Operated by an unnamed "proud member of the GCBRO," this site includes a photo gallery, list of suggested field research equipment, and an unfortunate number of typos ("Beleze" for "Belize," etc.). Even the GCBRO's title is misprinted as "Gulf South Bigfoot Reseach [sic] Organization."

► Bigfoot Field Researchers Organization

www.bfro.net

Often embroiled in controversy, and briefly disabled by hackers in 2013, the BFRO's website remains one of the most professional and diverse Internet sites devoted to all things Bigfoot. At press time for *Seeking Bigfoot*, its database of sightings included 5,216 reports from the United States, 284 from Canada, and 68 from other countries. Also included are links to French and German language blogs, numerous photographs and witness sketches, tips on collecting evidence, and critiques of rival hunters whom the BFRO's leaders regard as hoaxers. (Most of those return the favor by attacking the BFRO on their own websites.) The BFRO offers pay-as-you-go field excursions, priced between $300 and $500.

▶ Bigfoot Forums
http://bigfootforums.com
Offers links to various discussions, ranging from individual Bigfoot sightings (catalogued by US and Canadian regions, plus "Everywhere else!") to general cryptozoology.

▶ Bigfoot Hub
www.bigfoothub.com
An outdated clearinghouse for links to other blogs, articles, and video clips related to Bigfoot. The main page displayed a current date when visited in March 2014, but posted articles and announcements all dated from early 2010.

▶ Bigfoot Sightings
http://bigfootsightings.org
Site owner Linda Jo Martin lives near Happy Camp, California, some fifty miles from Bluff Creek. She holds membership in Friends of Sasquatch (see below), posting articles and editorials to her own site, in addition to photos and sighting reports from others around the country.

▶ Bigfoot Information Project
www.bigfootproject.org/index.html
While bearing a current copyright notice, this site appeared to be ten years behind the times when visited in early 2014. None of the articles or interviews posted is dated later than 2004.

▶ Bigfoot Lunch Club
www.bigfootlunchclub.com
Guy Edwards helms this informative and amusing site (note the "secret handshake" page), with announcements of Bigfoot-related events, corrections of published misinformation, an interactive world map of BHM sightings, and links to many other websites.

▶ BigFooT-Ohio
http://bftohio.blogspot.com
"Capt. Bligh" and "Chief Kerry" run this website and are responsible for the quirky spelling of "Bigfoot." "On the road" since 2011, the group—apparently consisting of three members, from the photograph online—may have cracked the time barrier, since Bligh's latest post!

▶ Bigfoot Research Center
www.bigfootresearchcenter.com
Operated by "a small private group of dedicated researchers who diligently collect evidence and partake in field research expeditions," the BRC apparently commenced operations in 2001, working primarily in the Olympic Mountains of Washington State, ranging farther afield in 2012 to British Columbia and Alaska. Its site includes expedition photos, videos, and audio recordings.

▶ Bigfoot Research Network

http://bigfootnetwork.tripod.com
Launched in 2000 as "a system to network and organize objective research efforts in the Eastern United States," the BRN website has not been updated since 2003.

▶ BigFoot Research Project Kentucky

http://bfrpky.com
Christopher Bennett and Brandon Lane comprise this group's membership, with colleague "John" left otherwise anonymous. Their site includes sighting reports and video and audio clips, with a list of field gear used by the hunters.

▶ Bigfoot Seekers

www.beyondtheveilparanormal.org/bigfootseekers
Founded in 2013, this "all women bigfoot research group" apparently consists of founding "core members" Dina Palazini, Kris Stepney, and Aryes Clague. The site includes video clips of their expeditions, witness interviews, and track finds.

Bigfoot statues abound along tourist routes in the Pacific Northwest. Credit: Author's collection.

▶ Bigfoot: The Beast of Kentucky

http://bigfootlore.blogspot.com
This site purports to "document Bigfoot reports and encounters and the history of bigfoot in Trimble, Carroll and Henry Counties of Kentucky and Eastern Kentucky." Having said that, its latest recorded sighting comes from Indiana, dated January 16, 2014 (see Chapter 2).

▶ Bigfoot Times

http://bigfoottimes.blogspot.com
Daniel Perez operates this website primarily as a vehicle for selling his *Bigfoot Times* newsletter, but also includes book reviews, vintage photos, and announcements of forthcoming exhibits.

▶ Bigfootology

http://bigfootology.com
President and chairman of the board Rhettman A. Mullis Jr. leads a no-kill

team of eight academic researchers and thirty-five diverse field representatives, including Justin Smeja (see Chapter 4), whose alleged slaying of two BHMs in 2010 goes unmentioned. "Non-team consultants" include Dr. John Bindernagel and Dr. Jeff Meldrum. A diverse site, ranging from sighting reports to merchandise offers and a "Hall of Fame" recognizing contributors to the field, Bigfootology is worth a look.

▶ Bigfoot's Blog
http://bigfootbooksblog.blogspot.com
Owner Steven Streufert describes his site as providing "Cryptic News from the Willow Creek View. Transhuman Sasquatch Strangeness from the Middle of Nowhere. A Voice Howling out from the Klamath-Trinity-Siskiyou Wilderness." Critiquing the published work of skeptics and Bigfoot believers alike, Streufert also directs potential customers to Bigfoot Books, his used-book shop in Willow Creek, California.

▶ Bill Green's New England Bigfoot Research Center
http://billgreen.weebly.com
Connecticut researcher Bill Green glimpsed Bigfoot from his apartment window in January 2005. His site focuses on reports from his home state (lifted from the BFRO), adding book and movie reviews.

▶ Bizarre Zoology
http://bizarrezoology.blogspot.com
Site owner Jay Cooney was a high school student when he launched this site in 2012, which makes it all the more amazing. For one so young, Jay has clearly done extensive networking and research, including attendance at Bigfoot symposiums, and his site is impressive by any standard.

▶ British Center for Bigfoot Research
http://british-bigfoot.tripod.com
While BHMs have been reported from Britain, this site—last updated in July 2002—lists only US sightings.

▶ British Columbia Scientific Cryptozoology Club
http://bcscc.ca/blog
A no-kill organization with an international membership, the BCSCC investigates various cryptids and publishes an informative quarterly newsletter. Its site includes an archive of articles dating from 2008, with various items of merchandise.

▶ Carolina Bigfoot Field Research
http://carolinabigfootfieldresearch.com
Site co-owners Dave Moser and David Pardue investigate reports from North and South Carolina, collaborating with Georgia "Bigfoot prospector" Rick Corliss to collect Peach State reports. Their site includes eyewitness reports, photos, video and audio clips.

▶ **Centre for Fortean Zoology**

www.cfz.org.uk.

Jonathan Downes leads the CFZ from his home in England, coordinating international expeditions in search of various cryptids. Presently the world's largest and most active cryptozoology organization, the CFZ maintains branches and websites in the US:
http://cfz-usa.blogspot.com, Canada
http://cfz-canada.blogspot.com/, Australia
www.cfzaustralia.com, and New Zealand
http://cfz-nz.blogspot.com.

▶ **Central Ohio Bigfoot Research**

http://blakemathys.com/sasquatch.html

While his uncle found and cast a seventeen-inch footprint in 1980, owner Blake Mathys warns visitors to his website that "I've never seen one of these creatures, and will not be convinced of their existence unless I do." Nonetheless, he remains interested and collects reports from other witnesses, dating from 1965 to March 2012, when the site was last updated.

▶ **Cryptomundo**

www.cryptomundo.com

Loren Coleman, John Kirk III, Rick Noll, and Craig Woolheater are the main contributors to this blog, billed as "a place to enjoy the adventures, treks, theories, and wisdom of some of the most respected leaders in the field of Cryptozoology." Aside from daily breaking news, the site also offers book reviews and selected "CryptoRama" merchandise.

▶ **Cryptoseekers Research**

http://cryptoseekersresearch.blogspot.com

Launched in 2009, this collection of "mini-blogs" covering BHM sightings from Florida has not been updated since April 2010.

The entrance to a "Bigfoot Walk" in North Bonneville, Washington, featuring hand-carved BHMs along its course.
Credit: Author's collection.

► Cryptozoonews

www.cryptozoonews.com

Loren Coleman runs this site, posting news items and photos as events and the spirit move him to do so.

► Delaware Bigfoot Center

http://delawarebigfootcenter.webs.com

Run by S. D. Anderson since its establishment in October 2012, this is a no-kill group confining its research to Delaware. The site includes several BHM sightings lifted from other organizations' online archives, a photo gallery, and the group's Articles of Formation.

► Desert Bigfoot

www.desertbigfoot.com

This is another no-kill group, concentrating on Bigfoot reports from Arizona. Leaders "Jeff," "John," and "Bernie" report possible ear-witness encounters with Bigfoot, but no personal sightings as of March 2014. Their site offers original reports from other witnesses, photos, video and audio clips, and a field research forum.

► East Tennessee Bigfoot

www.easttennesseebigfoot.org.

Matt Seeber founded this two-member group (with Ron Losey) in 2005, after his son saw Bigfoot in the family's backyard. The site includes a sightings database, photos, and an e-mail contact address for new sightings.

► Fathom Frontiers

www.fathomfrontiers.com

Active "for several years," this group of indeterminate size, led by "Jesse" and "Alan," claims fifteen Ohio expeditions and one in New York between June 2009 and July 2011. As *Seeking Bigfoot* went to press, no new entries had been posted to their blog since July 2013.

► Florida Bigfoot Researchers

www.floridabigfoot.com

This site was accessible online in March 2015, but opened with an undated statement reading: "After a 5 year quest to explore the bigfoot phenomenon, Florida Bigfoot Researches [*sic*] have determined adequate evidence is lacking to justify continued research with the hypothesis of the existence of a large bipedal hominin or ape-like creature in Florida."

A commemorative coin celebrating Florida's Skunk Ape. Credit: Author's collection.

▶ Florida Skunk Ape
www.floridaskunkape.com

Established by Dave Shealy in 1998, this site bills itself as "the official home and largest collection of Florida Skunk Ape sightings, reports, links and information on the Internet." It includes a database of sightings from the Sunshine State. A visit to the site in March 2014 revealed no items posted since May 2010.

▶ Frame 352: The Stranger Side of Sasquatch
http://paranormalbigfoot.blogspot.com

No-kill activist Regan Lee launched this blog—named for the most famous frame of Roger Patterson's 1967 film—in 2010, offering news, video clips, and controversial views on the relationship of BHMs to UFOs and other paranormal phenomena. Lee is open-minded. The results are either entertaining or infuriating, depending on a reader's point of view.

▶ Friends of Bigfoot
http://fob.l7space.com/index.php.

Run by managing editor Cliff Jones Sr., this site includes galleries of articles, photos, and audio and video clips, but is sadly out of date. Many of its links to other research groups are dead, and no "news" has been posted since April 2003.

▶ Friends of Sasquatch
http://friendsofsasquatch.com

This group claims two members but identifies only one: blogger/novelist Linda Jo Martin of Happy Camp, California. Advocating "psychic research" into BHMs, the site has not been updated since May 2012.

▶ Georgia Bigfoot Research & Investigation

www.gbriresearch.com/index.php/en

Founded by the late William Lamar Allen and wife Nancy (also deceased), the GBRI claims field research dating from 1962. The site lists Danny McClain as lead researcher from 1969 through 2004, with no successor identified.

▶ Georgia Bigfoot Society

http://georgiabigfootsociety.com

Led by director K. Steven Monk, the GBS commits itself to "understanding and protecting the Sasquatch People through extended encounters." The site offers new and out-of-print books for sale, includes a photo gallery, and provides a form for reporting BHM sightings.

▶ Greater Boston Bigfoot Research Institute

http://826boston.org/content/591

There's nothing to see here for BHM enthusiasts. Definitely not a Bigfoot research team, this group—also know as "826 Boston"—describes itself as "a nonprofit organization dedicated to supporting students ages 6–18 with their creative and expository writing skills, and to helping teachers inspire their students to write." Its online store offers a Bigfoot T-shirt and a "cryptozoology career starter kit" ("Coming Soon!"), sold to "help support free writing programs for students."

▶ Gulf Coast Bigfoot Research Organization

www.gcbro.com

Founded by Bobby Hamilton in 1997, the GCBRO welcomes members "who are either strong believers, or have had a Bigfoot encounter of their own, so there is no skepticism amongst any members of our group as far as the existence of these animals is concerned." Name notwithstanding, the group does not restrict collection of reports to the Deep South. As of March 2014 its database included sightings from forty-six US states, plus more from Canada, Australia, and Europe. The GCBRO offers a MonsterHunter Newsletter online.

▶ Idaho Bigfoot

http://idahobigfoot.com

Inspired by Theodore Roosevelt's 19th-century tale (see Chapter 1) and modern sightings, this site, while limited in content, includes several reports and some high-quality Bigfoot art.

▶ In Search of Orang Pendek

www.orangpendek.org.

Devoted to study of Indonesia's cryptic Orang Pendek ("short man"), this site, sadly, has not been updated since April 2008.

▶ Indiana Bigfoot Awareness Group
www.bigfoot46555.net
This no-kill group arose from a merger with the former Indiana Bigfoot Society, but its status and future are uncertain. Leader Walt Neice "currently isn't reachable via the Web," and a visit to the site in March 2014 found no information more recent than 2005.

▶ Iowa Bigfoot
www.iowabigfoot.com
Focused on Bigfoot reports from the Hawkeye State; this site has not been updated since December 2011.

▶ Kentucky Bigfoot Research Organization
http://kentuckybigfoot.com
Founded and led by high school teacher Charlie Raymond in 1997, the KBRO maintains an attractive, professional website with a database of Kentucky BHM reports current through February 2014 upon last examination. Other features include photos, video and audio clips, and a sighting submission form.

▶ Kiamichi Bigfoot Research
www.angelfire.com/ok5/kiamichibigfoot
This two-man, pro-kill group dedicates itself "to research and investigate Bigfoot/ Sasquatch in the Kiamichi Mountains of Southeastern Oklahoma." Its site includes an impressive photo gallery, but the most recent post on its message board dates from early January 2004.

▶ Kultus
www.kultusbook.com
This site is billed as "a companion blog to the novel," also titled *Kultus*, penned by author Kirk Sigurdson. Bigfoot appears on the novel's cover, and on this site, beside other quirky articles with headlines such as "PM of New Zealand Claims He's Not an Alien."

▶ Mad River Sasquatch Study
http://shadows-end0.tripod.com/MRSS.html
Focused on Bigfoot reports from Ohio, this site declared that "2010–2011 have proven to be very productive years for us, and we are eager to see what 2013 will yield," yet the last entry posted to its blog dates from August 2008. Still worth visiting, for researchers particularly interested in Buckeye sightings and/ or the Midwest at large.

▶ Michigan Bigfoot Research Blog
http://themichiganbigfootresearchblog.blogspot.com
This blog by Michigan researcher Nathaniel Bronis solicits Bigfoot sightings and reports on field expeditions, current through June 2013 at last viewing.

▶ Mid-America Bigfoot Research Center

www.mid-americabigfoot.com

Billed as a place "where researchers think outside the box," this site focuses primarily on sightings and Bigfoot-related events in Oklahoma. The most recent item posted, as of March 2014, dates from November 2013.

▶ Minnesota Bigfoot

www.minnesotabigfoot.com

Pledged to "investigate everything, assume nothing," this group seems to have shifted focus from its website (last updated in July 2012) to a Facebook page titled Squatch Inc. Sasquatch Research & Investigation.

▶ Mogollon Monster

http://mogollonmonster.com

Owned and operated by Mitchell Waite, this site promotes sales of his books and DVDs dealing with BHM reports from Arizona. Waite also offers "cryptozoology courses online" and a "national Bigfoot face database" collected to seek "matching faces from different times or places. A match will help identify real cryptids from the squatch blobs. This kind of data will be good for tracking migrations, longevity, clan associations, birth rates, and much more."

▶ Mother Son Research Team

http://oklahomabiggieinsearchfortruth.webs.com

A crime scene technician and her son, ten years old in 2010, comprise the membership of this team formed "in hopes to bring the Bigfoot community together." No forum or journal entries have been posted to the site since August 2010.

▶ Mysterious Australia

www.mysteriousaustralia.com

Run by Aussie author Rex Gilroy, Mysterious Australia describes itself as "one of those unique sites on the Internet that deals with the forgotten history of our continent including Anthropology, Archaeology, Cryptozoology, and Hominology, with an all Australasian Content!" That includes Yowie BHMs, plus mystery cats, aquatic cryptids, and other paranormal phenomena. Includes much useful information from Down Under, while promoting sales of books coauthored by Gilroy and wife Heather.

▶ Nevada Sasquatch

http://nevadasasquatch.blogspot.com

This website, paired with Sierra Tahoe Bigfoot Research (see below), is "devoted to the exploration of the possibility of an undiscovered bipedal homonid species making the Silver State their home." In March 2014 the page included sightings and video clips from December 2013.

▶ New Jersey Bigfoot Reporting Center

http://njbigfoot.org

Motivated by "a casual interest in all manner of spooky strangeness," Drew Vics created this site "as an effort to collect and archive possible New Jersey Bigfoot sightings for research purposes and to serve as a general repository of New Jersey sighting reports as reference for others with an interest in Bigfoot." Reports on file span the years from 1894 to 2013.

▶ North American Bigfoot

www.northamericanbigfoot.com

Cliff Barackman's blog promotes the *Finding Bigfoot* TV series, presents a gallery of footprint casts dating from 1960, instructional videos for would-be Bigfoot trackers, and much more.

▶ North America Bigfoot Search

www.nabigfootsearch.com/home.html

David Paulides founded this website in 2004, "to offer the visitor a unique and bias free view of the bipeds [*sic*] world." Controversy surrounds its support for habituation and defense of hoaxer Ray Wallace. Also offers information on missing persons with "a historical aspect to this issue and...common elements that run through the disappearances."

▶ North American Wood Ape Conservancy

http://woodape.org

Active since 1999 under various names (see Chapter 3), the NAWAC presently investigates Bigfoot reports from Arkansas, Louisiana, Oklahoma and Texas. Its site includes field reports, a photo gallery, and membership applications.

▶ North America's Great Ape: The Sasquatch

www.bigfootbiologist.org

Site owner Dr. John Bindernagel presents eyewitness descriptions and drawings, footprint casts and photographs, and other evidence such as unexplained damage to trees, while discussing possible confusion of bears with Bigfoot.

▶ North East Sasquatch Researchers Association

www.teamnesra.net/drupal

According to this site, "The NESRA team is a group of everyday people from all walks of life who share a common interest in Bigfoot and specialize in field research." While not explicitly no-kill, one spokesman writes, "I guess in the end I see a great deal of selfish motive in those who want one dead, because somewhere in the end a creature has to die likely due to someone's underlying profit motive."

▶ North East Washington Bigfoot Researchers Unlimited

www.povn.com/mtnmama

Interested in Bigfoot since 1967 and convinced of its existence by discovery of a sixteen-inch footprint in 1998, Leonard Stigall Sr. formed this group with wife Doris and others to conduct field research. Website content is limited to introducing team members.

▶ Northern Sasquatch Research Society

www.northernbigfoot.net

The site includes a statement of principles (belief in Bigfoot, "wonder" that it shares our world, commitment to protect the species) and a small photo gallery. Despite its limited content, navigation between its pages proved awkward on my visit.

▶ Ohio Bigfoot Organization

http://ohiobigfootorganization.blogspot.com

Apparently a four-member group, the OBO may now be defunct. The last dated entry on its website bears the headline "It's Going to be a Big year in 2011."

▶ Olympic Project

www.olympicproject.com/index.html

This group collaborated in Dr. Melba Ketchum's DNA study (see Chapter 5) and planned a field expedition with Dr, Jeff Meldrum in March 2014, including classes on field research for beginners. Controversy surrounds the DNA findings and the group's support for Justin Smeja (Chapter 4). Photo galleries included.

▶ Ohio/Pennsylvania Bigfoot Research Group

http://sasquatchsearch.tripod.com

While still accessible online, this site was last updated in August 2004. Its parent group, formed in 1978, existed "to research, seek, and investigate the Bigfoot phenomenon in Ohio and Pennsylvania in an objective, scientific manner to find the truth."

▶ Oregon Bigfoot

www.oregonbigfoot.com

Founded by Autumn Williams, the site remains active despite her announced retirement from active research. Title notwithstanding, the site's database includes an interactive map of the US with Bigfoot reports from most states, plus a similar map of Oregon permitting research by counties. An impressive resource.

▶ Our Bigfoot

www.ourbigfoot.com

Take the title literally for this site, which reports one anonymous family's interaction with local BHMs since 1956 but also includes much general information and an extensive article archive.

▶ Ozarks Bigfoot

http://ozarksbigfoot.com

This self-described "independent group researching the folklore and history of Bigfoot in the Ozarks" claims two decades of experience and plans the release of a documentary film in 2014. The website offers historical background, photos, video and audio clips, and a map of sighting reports.

A T-shirt logo recognizing Bigfoot as a symbol of Oregon.
Credit: Author's collection.

▶ Pennsylvania Bigfoot Society

www.pabigfootsociety.com

A committed no-kill group, the PBA reports recent sightings and offers an interactive state map searchable by county for older reports. Archives include historical articles, photos, maps, and video and audio clips.

▶ Pennsylvania Research Organization

www.paresearchers.com

Sharing turf with the PBS, this husband-wife team of paranormal researchers includes Bigfoot on the list of mysterious phenomena, with such conventional topics as wildlife and archaeology. The site includes a Bigfoot sighting database.

▶ Pinellas Pasco Paranormal

www.pinellaspascoparanormal.com/floridabigfoot.htm

While describing themselves as "hostile haunt specialists," the team also includes Bigfoot sightings and photos on its website, with the proviso that they "will not work with, assist or give any information to any Bigfoot hunting group, that comes to Florida to capture, kill, or even harass the Florida Bigfoot.... Given how hot the quest for a Bigfoot body has become, right now we do not trust any of the Bigfoot hunting/research teams whatsoever at this point."

▶ Sasquatch Bigfoot Research Unit

www.freewebs.com/sasquatchbigfootresearchunit

Founded in 2002, with headquarters in Greencastle, Indiana, the SBRU claims "members from numerous states." The website was last updated in November 2006 by lead investigators Austin Hutchison and Tyler Vance.

▶ Sasquatch Bioacoustic
http://sites.google.com/site/mongahela
A website devoted entirely to purported Bigfoot vocalizations, Sasquatch Bioacoustic is "dedicated to supporting this line of research and offers a growing catalog of unknown vocal and non-vocal audio clips. These audio recordings are assembled and characterized here to foster a growing knowledge of the vocals most frequently encountered by this research community and to aid others who may encounter similar vocals when in the field." Definitely worth a look—and a listen.

▶ Sasquatch Canada
www.sasquatchcanada.com
Bigfoot recognizes no borders, and neither does the Internet. Owned and operated by Candy Michlosky, this site calls itself "your #1 resource center for all things Sasquatch." While that may overstate the case, it offers photos and video clips, BHM sightings by province, a list of recommended reading—and a real estate offer of "Bigfoot property for sale."

▶ Sasquatch Genome Project
http://sasquatchgenomeproject.org
The official online home of Dr. Melba Ketchum's controversial Bigfoot DNA study (Chapter 5), this site examines the case in microscopic detail and answers objections from various critics.

▶ Sasquatch in British Columbia
http://sasquatch-bc.com
Owned by a group called West Coast Sasquatch Research, founded in 2004, this site strikes a pose of objectivity: "We'll supply the perspective. You supply your own conclusion!" It offers short biographies of leading researchers, book reviews, and a photo gallery.

▶ Sasquatch Hunters
http://thesasquatchhunters.com
Founders Stacy Brown Sr. and Jr. collaborate with investigators in Florida and Georgia "to educate people on the topic of Sasquatch through first hand experience." While no members are listed beyond the states named, the group offers pay-as-you-go "weekend excursions in an area near you"—including North Carolina, New York, and Pennsylvania—at $500 per head. Caveat emptor.

▶ Sasquatch Information Society
www.bigfootinfo.org
Founded by Robert Murdock, the site includes a database of Bigfoot sightings from various places in the US and Canada, a photo gallery, and products offered for sale. Its "Research Tools" page is "a work in progress."

▶ Sasquatch Investigations of the Rockies
http://sasquatchinvestigations.org
Founded by Michael Johnson and Scott Barta, the SIR bills itself as "the only Bigfoot research group whose origins are in Colorado.... All our evidence is from Colorado and it is our own." That evidence includes an extensive photo gallery and video clips, sharing space with a page of SIR merchandise.

▶ Sasquatch Research Association
http://sasquatchresearchers.org
The SRA's motto is "Don't believe, know." Based in Minneapolis, Minnesota, its goal is "to provide information on the North American Sasquatch/Bigfoot, a community forum, and a central repository of collected evidence and vetted eye witness accounts of Sasquatch sightings across North America to aid the efforts of those people legitimately researching and accruing evidence of this elusive creature." The site includes photos and field reports.

▶ Sasquatch Tracker
http://sasquatchtracker.com
Another regional website, this one calls itself "Alaska's cryptid authority since 2005." Owner M. Charlie Thompson describes himself as "a private and independent researcher currently concentrating my search for Sasquatch in the northern frontier of Alaska. The primary focus of my research, field investigation and expeditions are in the interior of Alaska and the border area of the Yukon Territory."

▶ Sasquatch Watch of Montana
http://montanabigfoot.weebly.com/index.html
Pete Wilson leads this no-kill "Bigfoot and wildlife scientific field research group." His site was still under construction as of March 2014.

▶ Sasquatch Watch of Virginia
www.sasquatchwatch.org
When visited in March 2014, this site—launched by director Billy Willard in 2005—led off with an introductory paragraph identical to that of the Montana site described above. The SWV's site includes an interactive map of Virginia sightings by county (linked to reports on the BFRO's website) and reports on the group's expeditions.

▶ Sasqwatch
http://bigfootwatch.com
This site is devoted to sale of the "Sasqwatch," a novelty wristwatch in the form of a hominid foot, with Bigfoot's revolving arms indicating the time. "It's no hoax!"—but it does cost $24.95 plus shipping and handling. Spare "feet" in various colors ($5.95 each) "help you adapt to the environment of your next Bigfoot search!"

▶ Search for the Maryland Bigfoot

www.oocities.org/marylandbigfoot/Main.html

This site provides a basic history of sightings in Maryland and a handful of modern reports, with the most recent dating from January 2004. Several links to other sightings were dead in March 2014.

▶ Searching for Bigfoot

www.searchingforbigfoot.com

Owned by "The Real Bigfoot Hunter, Tom Biscardi" (see Chapter 4), this website promotes his work, including an as-yet-untitled future "fictional, pseudo documentary, found footage style Bigfoot movie. Get Ready World!" Enough said.

▶ ShukerNature

http://karlshuker.blogspot.com

Moving from the bizarre to the sublime, this is the blog of Dr. Karl Shuker, rightful heir to the mantle of Dr. Bernard Heuvelmans as the world's preeminent cryptozoology author. While you're in the neighborhood, check out his personal website at www.karlshuker.com, which includes the best bibliography available on all things cryptid.

▶ Sierra Tahoe Bigfoot Research

http://sierratahoebigfoot.blogspot.com

This website, "dedicated to the research of Bigfoot, and its habitat, in the Tahoe and outlying Sierra region of Nevada and California," is paired with the Nevada Bigfoot site (see above). It reports recent sightings in the target area and offers merchandise for sale.

▶ Sierras Evidence Initiative

www.sierrasiteproject.com

Bart Cutino and Justin Smeja operate this site, promoting Smeja's tale of killing Bigfoot (Chapter 4). Other Team Sierras members include Ro Sahebi, Tyler Huggins, and Shawn Evidence (yes, seriously).

▶ Sierra Sasquatch

www.sierrasasquatch.com/index.html

Site owner and registered nurse Jaime Avalos claims a Bigfoot sighting from June 2006, sparking his quest. In addition to personal field expeditions, he offers a $10,000 reward "for the positive identification of the track makers in the Sierra Nevadas."

▶ Skunk Ape Research Headquarters

www.skunkape.info

Dave Shealy maintains this site, promoting his work and his Trail Lakes Campground in Ochopee, Florida. The site includes a photo gallery and gift shop, but did not feature Shealy's purported Skunk Ape videos when visited in March 2014 (although a DVD is sold for $19).

▶ Smokey and the Fouke Monster

www.smokeycrabtree.com

Established by the late Smokey Crabtree, author of three books dealing with the Arkansas version of Bigfoot, this site remains online, offering those works and other merchandise despite his death in April 2011.

▶ SnowWalkerPrime

www.youtube.com/user/SnowWalkerPrime

Devoted to "tracking the Great Beast in the wilds of Maine," this blog features various video clips posted by site owner "Michael."

Dave Shealy's Skunk Ape Research Headquarters in the Florida Everglades. Credit: Author's collection.

▶ South Carolina Bigfoot
http://southcarolinabigfoot-jodie.blogspot.com
Blogger "Jodie" reports visits from a presumed BHM between November 2011 and November 2012, when he or she ceased posting updates.

▶ Southeast Sasquatch Association
http://southeastsasquatchassociation.blogspot.com
This blog provides announcements of forthcoming events and many links to other websites.

▶ Squatchdetective's Blog
http://squatchdetective.wordpress.com
Providing news and commentary from Steve Kulls, fact-checking rival Bigfoot researchers, and archiving episodes of Squatchdetective Radio.

▶ Stan Courtney Sasquatch Listening Project
www.stancourtney.com/wordpress
Another website dealing primarily with presumed Bigfoot vocalizations. Some are available for listening online, others sold on CD.

▶ Stocking Hominid Research Inc.
www.stockinghominidr.com
President Diane Stocking and Vice President Ron Schaffner pledge themselves "to the scientific pursuit of knowledge and classification of Hominids typically known as Sasquatch, Bigfoot, and Skunk Ape." They accept donations toward that goal, while offering photos, maps, and audio clips.

▶ Sylvanic
www.sylvanic.com
Founded in 2005 by "a biologist from Great Falls, Montana; a Cree Nations elder representing the First Nations People; the skeptic Todd Standing; and a paramedic fire fighter from Calgary, Alberta," the Sylvanic group has produced several intriguing videos of purported BHMs. The group claims "tremendous success…from our enormous collaboration of minds, experiences, knowledge, and wisdom from all walks of life."

▶ TEXLA Cryptozoological Research Group
www.texlaresearch.com/index.html
This group collects Bigfoot reports and supporting evidence from East Texas, southeastern Oklahoma, and Louisiana. Its website features audio recordings, information on suspected Bigfoot hair, and "how-to" lessons for would-be monster hunters.

► **ThomSquatch**

www.thomsquatch.com

This blog belongs to author/researcher Thom Powell (see Chapter 3), presenting articles by and about its owner.

► **Tim the Yowie Man**

www.yowieman.com.au

Another website dealing with the Australian version of Bigfoot, this one is operated by Tim "The Yowie Man" Bull, arguably the best-known Aussie cryptozoologist besides Rex Gilroy. The site includes photos, media reports, and links to Bull's radio broadcasts.

► **TriState Bigfoot**

www.tristatebigfoot.com

Active since 2009 and calling itself "Ohio's top ranked Bigfoot team website," TriState Bigfoot also collects reports from Indiana and Kentucky. The site indeed includes case files from Ohio and Kentucky ("none available" from Indiana, as of March 2014), while offering property investigations and public presentations at no charge.

An Australian press report of a modern Yowie sighting. Credit: Author's collection.

► **United Bigfoot Research Group**

www.ubrg.org

Claiming fifty-seven active members, the UBRG is a no-kill organization seeking to "educate both members and the public on current findings in bigfoot research." Its site includes a photo gallery, audio clips, articles written by members, and a roster of state wildlife protection statutes.

► **Unknown Explorers**

www.unknownexplorers.com/index.php

This is an all-purpose paranormal website, including cryptozoological information with hauntings, UFO reports, etc.

► **Utah Bigfoot**

www.utahbigfoot.blogspot.com

This site consists of a photographic essay on areas where BHMs have been reported statewide.

▶ Virginia Bigfoot Research Organization

www.virginiabigfootresearch.org

Pledged to "combining scientific methodology and shamanistic awareness in hopes of establishing peaceful contact" with Bigfoot, this site lists BHM reports from various counties, with audio clips and media articles.

▶ Visits from the Forest People

www.bigfootbook.net

Author Julie Scott created this site to promote her book of the same title. It includes an overview of the text, with reviews and photo galleries.

▶ Washington Sasquatch Research Team

www.wasrt.com

Led by Steve Wilkins and Steve Schauer, this group has conducted research in Washington State since June 2010, with its latest post dating from December 2013. The site includes photos and video clips, with a timeline of the group's research activities.

▶ West Texas Bigfoot Research

http://westtexasbigfootresearch.freeservers.com

Rory Heaton of Odessa, Texas, established this site "to show and prove that Bigfoot can and does live in West Texas and to show pictures from the research that I'm doing." He includes a photo gallery and information on a sighting from May 2004.

▶ West Virginia Bigfoot Investigations Group

http://steventitchenell.tripod.com

President Steven Titchenell founded this organization in April 2006, listing its dual objectives as "to resolve the mystery of Bigfoot and if it's determined they do exist, to study their movements, diet, and other behaviors without causing any harm to them." When checked in March 2014 the site listed thirty-one reported sightings, with six of those debunked. Audio clips are also included.

▶ West Virginia Bigfoot Research Association

http://westvirginiabigfoot.blogspot.com

This site, established by Rick Skeen and last updated in August 2012, includes a photo gallery with reports of BHM sightings.

▶ Wilkes Bigfoot Research

www.wilkesbigfootresearch.com

Ricky Lunsford of Wilkes, North Carolina, established this Web page in 2011, belatedly motivated by a personal sighting in 1979 and a near-fatal illness in 2010. His sparse site provides one newspaper clipping on his own experience, with links to other Web pages.

► Wisconsin Bigfoot

www.wisconsinbigfoot.com

Last updated in July 2012, this website suggests techniques for monster hunters, lists several Wisconsin reports, with media articles, photos, audio and video clips. Its activity has apparently shifted to Facebook, at Squatch Inc. Sasquatch Research & Investigation (see below).

► Yowie: In Search of Australia's Bigfoot

www.yowiefile.com

This site promotes and updates the best-ever book on Australia's resident BHM, adding valuable new information.

Bigfoot Meets Facebook

Facebook pages, as any subscriber must know, are prone to digression, disputes, and what were once called "flame wars" in earlier cyber-times (say, five years ago). Bigfoot/Sasquatch-related pages are listed alphabetically here, with emphasis on groups or individuals engaged in research or discussion, without endorsement, permitting readers to pick and choose for themselves. Simply type the page's name as shown into the "Find" slot on your Facebook page. As an alternative, type in "Bigfoot" and/or "Sasquatch" alone, and brace yourself!

- ► Albemarle Sasquatch Society
- ► Alberta Sasquatch
- ► Alliance of Independent Bigfoot Researchers
- ► American Society of Christian Bigfoot Believers
- ► Appalachian Bigfoot Reporting
- ► Aquatic Sasquatch Society
- ► Bigfoot Believers
- ► Bigfoot Declassified
- ► Bigfoot Discovery Museum
- ► Bigfoot Enigma
- ► Bigfoot Evidence News
- ► Bigfoot Field Guide TV
- ► Bigfoot Field Reporter
- ► Bigfoot Field Researchers Organization
- ► Bigfoot Finder
- ► Bigfoot Hotspot Radio
- ► Bigfoot in Art History
- ► Bigfoot in Maryland
- ► Bigfoot in the CSRA [Central Savannah River Area]
- ► Bigfoot in the New Jersey 'Burbs
- ► Bigfoot Lunch Club
- ► Bigfoot Observation Group
- ► Bigfoot of the Uwharries
- ► Bigfoot Recon
- ► Bigfoot Recordings by Ron Morehead
- ► Bigfoot Research News
- ► Bigfoot Research Organization
- ► Bigfoot Research Society
- ► Bigfoot Researchers of the Hudson Valley
- ► Bigfoot Sasquatch Talk
- ► Bigfoot Seekers
- ► Bigfoot Sightings
- ► Bigfoot South Dakota

- Bigfoot Stories
- Bigfoot: The Evidence
- Bigfoot United
- British & Europe Bigfoot Research
- California Native Entities and Bigfoot Forum
- CFZ—Centre for Fortean Zoology
- Colorado Bigfoot Research
- Delaware Sasquatch Research Institute
- Dr. Jeff Meldrum—Project Sasquatch
- DWS Bigfoot Researchers
- East Tennessee Bigfoot
- Fans of Bigfoot
- Find Bigfoot
- Forbidden Bigfoot
- Illinois Bigfoot Research Society
- Ken Gerhard (Cryptozoologist)
- Kentucky Bigfoot Research Organization
- Looking For Bigfoot
- Maine Bigfoot Society
- Meigs County's "White Bigfoot"
- Michigan Sasquatch Investigation Team
- Mid-America Bigfoot Research Center
- Midwest Investigations Sasquatch Team
- Midwestern Developmental Discovery of Sasquatch Society
- Minnesota Bigfoot Research Team
- Missouri Bigfoot Hunters
- Mountain State Sasquatch Watch
- New England Bigfoot Organization
- New York Bigfoot Society
- NjBigfoot [New Jersey sightings]
- North Alabama Sasquatch
- North American Bigfooters
- North American Sasquatch Association
- North American Sasquatch Bigfoot Researchers Organization
- Northeast Ohio Bigfoot
- Northwest Bigfoot
- Ohio Bigfoot Conference
- Ohio Bigfoot Hunters
- Oklahoma Bigfoot Symposium
- Oklahoma Sasquatch Hunters
- Operation Bigfoot
- Oregon Sasquatch Symposium
- Pennsylvania Bigfoot Association

- Pennsylvania Bigfoot Field Research Association
- Pennsylvania Bigfoot Investigations
- Pennsylvania Bigfoot Society
- Pennsylvania Sasquatch Association
- Portland Sasquatch Research Project
- Salt Fork Sasquatch Encounters
- Sasquatch ATV Research Team
- Sasquatch Brotherhood
- Sasquatch Club of Northern Vermont
- Sasquatch Daily
- Sasquatch Evidence
- Sasquatch Hunter
- Sasquatch Inc. Sasquatch Research & Investigation
- Sasquatch Information Society
- Sasquatch People
- Sasquatch Preservation Association of North Carolina
- Sasquatch Report
- Sasquatch Research Center
- Sasquatch Research Institute
- SasquatchResearch.net
- Sasquatch Research Team: Polk County, Georgia
- SasquatchScoop.com
- Sasquatch Society
- Sasquatch Summit
- Sasquatch Watch
- Sasquatch Watch Canada
- Sasquatch Watch of Virginia
- Sasquatch Watch Radio
- Searching for Bigfoot
- Searching for Sasquatch
- Sierra Sasquatch
- SIR-Sasquatch Investigations of The Rockies
- Southeastern Bigfoot Research Group
- SouthEastern Ohio Society for Bigfoot Investigation
- Southern Appalachian Bigfoot Conference
- Southern Oregon Bigfoot
- Southern Sasquatch Research Organization
- Southwestern Virginia Bigfoot Research and Investigation
- Squatch Inc. Sasquatch Research & Investigation
- Squatchermetrics - The PNW Sasquatch

- State of Jefferson Sasquatch Research
- Tennessee Bigfoot
- Texas Bigfoot Research Center
- Texas Bigfoot Research Conservancy
- The Bigfoot Forums
- The Bigfoot Report
- The Keystone Bigfoot Project
- The Sasquatch Hunters.com
- The Sasquatch People
- Timberline Bigfoot
- Timberline Bigfoot's Sasquatch Unlimited
- TriState Bigfoot
- Utah Bigfoot Research Center
- Uwharrie Mountain Bigfoot
- Vermont Sasquatch Researchers
- Virginia Bigfoot Conference
- Walker County Bigfoot Research Organization
- Walla Walla Bigfoot
- Washington Sasquatch Research Team
- West Virginia Bigfoot
- West Virginia Bigfoot Investigation Team
- West Virginia Bigfoot Investigations Group
- West Virginia Bigfoot Research
- Wisconsin Sasquatch

Newsgroups

Scores of Internet newsgroups exist—at least in theory—devoted to Bigfoot and its kin. Regardless of their size or inactivity, they remain listed forever, it seems, and even the most active may wither and vanish overnight. Those listed below were "active" at press time for *Seeking Bigfoot*, claiming multiple members and messages posted within the past six months. To connect, search by the group's name after Googling "Yahoo groups."

- Adirondack Bigfoot Club
- Appalachian Mountains Bigfoot Research
- Big Foot Hunters of Ohio
- Bigfoot [Loren Coleman's newsgroup]
- Bigfoot Buddies
- Bigfoot Mystery
- Bigfoot Newsletter Online
- Bigfoot Ranger Team
- Bigfoot Research of the Northeast
- Bigfoot Tracker
- Chupacabra
- Cryptolist
- CryptoSearch
- Forest Giants
- Frontiers of Zoology
- Georgia Bigfoot Society
- Michigan Bigfoot Investigators
- North American Bigfooters Club
- North Carolina Bigfoot Sightings
- North Carolina Unexplained
- Ohio/Pennsylvania Bigfoot
- Paranormal California
- Paranormal Florida
- Sasquatch Watch of Virginia
- Unexplained Georgia
- Washington State Sasquatch

CHAPTER 8

MONSTER MEDIA

Bigfoot is everywhere you look these days, unless you're searching in the woods. On television, YouTube, and in feature films—even in "death metal" music—BHMs are inescapable. This chapter lists, summarizes, and reviews various twenty-first-century media offerings relevant to Bigfoot and its kin, whether played straight, for laughs, or as a vehicle for thrills and chills.

BooTube

The Internet's video-sharing YouTube website swarms with film and video clips related to Bigfoot, including excerpts from feature films and TV series, amateur videos of purported monster sightings, interviews with witnesses, and dedicated pages maintained by various researchers. Some—by no means all—of the clips available at press time were listed under the following titles (alphabetized for convenience):

Abducted by Bigfoot

- A Closer Look—Bigfoot Caught on Dash Cam
- A Closer Look—Bigfoot Filmed Independence Day
- A Closer Look—Possible Tricopter Bigfoot Footage at Salt Fork park
- A Nonchalant Sighting in Utah— Finding Bigfoot: Rejected Evidence
- Bigfoot and the Men in Black
- Bigfoot and the Military
- Bigfoot and Sasquatch Encounters Across America
- Bigfoot and Strange Disappearances
- Bigfoot Attacks Scientists in Canada Documentary
- Bigfoot: Class A Sighting Witness Interview
- Bigfoot Encounter—Bigfoot Shot— Exclusive! Never Told Until Now!
- Bigfoot Found and Killed!
- Bigfoot in Arizona The Howler
- Bigfoot in Mr. Mike's Backyard New 2014
- Bigfoot Kill Photo Examination
- Bigfoot Lurking on the Hillside
- Bigfoot: New Evidence & Footage Emerging
- Bigfoot Santa Cruz Captured
- Bigfoot Sighting Bradford Pennsylvania October 2013
- Big Foot Sighting "Hi Deff "
- Bigfoot Sighting in Washington State
- Bigfoot Sighting Mendocino County 1970—Bigfoot Strides by Remote Cabin
- Bigfoot Sighting Traumatizes Turkey Hunter
- Bigfoot Stalking Campers In Arizona
- Bigfoot: The Definitive Guide
- Bigfoot Throws Log at Camper
- Bigfoot Tracker Rick Dyer Talking About the Dead Bigfoot
- Biker Chased by Bigfoot in Ontario Canada
- Calgary Bigfoot—Stabilized, Zoomed, Enhanced
- Close Encounters with Bigfoot
- Documentary On Native Americans And Bigfoot
- Finding Bigfoot
- First Bigfoot Medical Evidence Released and Explained by San Antonio Medical Doctor
- Full Footage! Massive Bigfoot Caught on Thermal!
- Grays Harbour Bigfoot Investigation w/ Jonathan Brown SLP2-6
- Hunter Films Possible Bigfoot From Blind
- Investigators Encounter Bigfoot in

the Redwoods of California
- ► Jeff Meldrum on Dyer's Bigfoot
- ► Large Sasquatch Caught on Video in Alberta!
- ► Lori & Dustin Chandler's Bigfoot Encounters
- ► Marble Mountain Bigfoot "Original Video"
- ► Massive Bigfoot Stalking Man and His Dogs
- ► Mike Wooley's Terrifying Bigfoot encounter
- ► Mink Creek Idaho Bigfoot
- ► Native American & Bigfoot
- ► New Bigfoot Photo From Oklahoma!
- ► Real Sasquatch Filmed In Sask. You Don't Want to Miss This One!
- ► Russian Boys Film Bigfoot/Yeti Carrying a Baby
- ► Sasquatch Fight Broken Up By Incredibly Massive Sasquatch!!
- ► Sasquatch in Rangeley, Maine
- ► Sasquatch Ontario
- ► Sasquatch Seen On Vancouver Island BC
- ► Sylvanic Bigfoot Killings
- ► The Bigfoot Body Uncut and Explained
- ► The Bigfoot Creatures of Ohio
- ► The Search for Bigfoot Type Creatures in Kentucky Documentary
- ► The Unseen Tribes "Best Bigfoot Documentary Ever"
- ► Treepeeking Sasquatch
- ► Woman Claims to Live in Cave With Bigfoot
- ► Woman Spots Bigfoot In Colorado Very Credible Incident
- ► Woman Takes a Photo of a Sasquatch While Hiking!!
- ► And so on, for seventy-four closely-spaced pages of listings. Feel free to browse!

Small Screen Sasquatchery

Bigfoot took commercial television by storm in the early twenty-first century. Midway through the new millennium's second decade, BHMs had colonized half a dozen networks and spawned a series of hilarious commercials on the side.

First off the mark, from Australia, was *Animal X*, premiering in 1997 with twenty-six half-hour episodes, each including three shorter segments on various cryptids and other animal wonders, such as "dolphin therapy," rains of fish, and a "hypnotizing dog." Aired in more than 120 countries through the latter 1990s, *Animal X* broadcast vignettes on Bigfoot, Yeti, Yowie, and Maryland's "goatman" before Animal Planet picked it up in the United States. Animal Planet teamed with the BFRO for an expedition in Washington State, uncovering the controversial "Skookum cast" in September 2000 (see Chapter 5), which rated a full episode of its own three months later. Today, the series survives as the *Animal X Natural Mystery Unit*, offering ten one-hour episodes compiled from past broadcasts.

Sasquatch: Legend Meets Science lit the fuse for the modern Bigfoot explosion in January 2003. Aired on the Discovery Channel as a two-hour documentary, the program featured scientists from various disciplines reviewing evidence that included footprints, the Skookum body cast (see Chapter 5), audio recordings, the Patterson film, and more recent video clips. Dr. Jeffrey Meldrum published a companion book to the special, and a DVD sold online expands the original program, including a new photo gallery.

Mysterious Encounters, hosted by researcher Autumn Williams, followed close behind the Discovery special, airing on the Outdoor Life Channel between September 2003 and January 2004. Unlike some other "monster" series, *Mysterious Encounters* focused solely on Bigfoot. Its thirteen episodes included: "Florida Skunk Ape" (first broadcast on September 27), "Alabama Booger Monster" (October 4), "Louisiana Swamp Creature" (October 11), "The Creature of Whitehall" (October 18), "Creature of Cumberland" (October 25), "Mount St. Helens" (November 1), "Mountain Devil" (November 15), "Tsiako Beast" (November 22), "California Creek Devil" (November 29), "Bigfoot of Bluff Creek, CA" (December 6), "Oklahoma Wildman" (December 13), "Redwood Forest Giant" (December 20), and "Texas Thicket Monster" (January 24, 2004).

▶ **MonsterQuest**, broadcast on the History Channel between October 2007 and March 2010, took a more eclectic view of cryptozoology, pursuing various unknown creatures around the world, but BHMs monopolized fifteen of its sixty-eight episodes spanning four seasons. Those episodes included:

Video cover for season three of *MonsterQuest*.
Credit: Author's collection.

- ▶ **"Sasquatch Attack" (November 7, 2007), examining reports of aggressive BHMs in Northern Ontario and the Pacific Northwest.**
- ▶ **"Bigfoot" (November 28, 2007), continuing investigations in Washington State and featuring a digital enhancement of the Patterson film.**
- ▶ **"Swamp Beast" (December 26, 2007), seeking skunk apes in the marshes of Florida and Louisiana.**
- ▶ **"Ohio Grassman" (June 18, 2008), pursuing the Buckeye State's version of Bigfoot.**
- ▶ **"Legend of the Hairy Beast" (July 30, 2008), reviewing Native American legends of forest giants.**
- ▶ **"China's Wildman"(September 21, 2008), visiting the Far East in search of the hairy biped known as Yeren.**
- ▶ **"Sasquatch Attack II" (November 12, 2008), recapping details from the previous episode on Bigfoot aggression toward humans, with new DNA evidence from bloodstains found at one scene.**
- ▶ **"Swamp Stalker" (February 18, 2009), tracking the Fouke Monster of Arkansas made famous in 1972 by The Legend of Boggy Creek.**

- ▶ "Snowbeast Slaughter" (March 11, 2009), penetrating the Rocky Mountains after ranchers blame a BHM for killing their livestock and wild elk.
- ▶ "Monster Close Encounters" (March 25, 2009), recounting a series of Bigfoot sightings reported from Minnesota to Washington State.
- ▶ "Mysterious Ape Island" (April 29, 2009), seeking BHMs on British Columbia's Vancouver Island.
- ▶ "Critical Evidence" (July 8, 2009), applying state-of-the-art technology and scientific analysis to the perceived best evidence of Bigfoot's existence.

- ▶ "Abominable Snowman" (October 25, 2009), a special two-hour episode investigating reports of the Himalayan Yeti, later released as part of the History Channel's *In Search of History* DVD series.
- ▶ "Hillbilly Beast" (January 20, 2010), tracking eyewitness reports, strange vocalizations, and a mysterious tooth from the mountains of northwestern Kentucky.
- ▶ "Sierra Sasquatch" (March 17, 2010), tracing Bigfoot reports in California's Sierra Nevada range from Native American legends to a 1991 videotape shot at Mono Lake.

▶ Next in line came **Destination Truth**, first aired on the SyFy network (known as "Sci-Fi" at the time) on June 6, 2007. The show's fifth season ended on August 7, 2012, with the show's cancellation announced in March 2014. Like *MonsterQuest* before it, *Destination Truth* traveled the world in search of cryptids, adding ghosts and demons to permit cross-pollination with the network's popular *Ghost Hunters* series. Unlike the competition, though, DT was helmed by host Josh Gates, with a cast of expedition members changing over time. The program's BHM-related episodes include:

Advertisement for *Destination Truth*, picturing team leader Josh Gates. Credit: Author's collection.

- ▶ "Bigfoot & Nahuelito" (first aired on June 27, 2007), dividing the episode between a search for apemen in Malaysia's Endau Rompin National Park and fishing for an Argentinean lake monster.
- ▶ "The Yeti" (March 5, 2008), taking Gates and company to Nepal in search of the so-called Abominable Snowman, procuring a new footprint cast.
- ▶ "Wild Man & Swamp Dinosaur" (March 19, 2008), dividing time between Cambodian BHMs and Africa's elusive Mokele-mbembe.

- ▶ "The Yowie & Haunted Mosque" (September 3, 2008), taking the team Down Under in search of Bigfoot's Aussie cousin, then rebounding to Malaysia for a ghost hunt.
- ▶ "Orang Pendek & Worm Monster" (September 10, 2008), pursuing Sumatra's legendary "short man" and a cryptid dwelling in Iceland's Lake Lagarfljót.
- ▶ "King Tut's Curse/Swamp Ape" (September 23, 2009), braving the sands of Egypt before plunging into Florida's Big Cypress National Preserve to seek Skunk Apes.

- "The Bhutan Yeti" (November 4, 2009), round two with the Snowman in a new setting, this time bagging hair samples with DNA from "an unknown primate."
- "The Jersey Devil/The Yeren" (March 31, 2010), visiting China's Hubei province in the second half-hour, seeking its resident "wild man."
- "Siberian Snowman" (October 7, 2010), trekking across the tundra in search of the Almas, Central Asia's version of the Yeti.
- "Vietnam's Bigfoot" (July 10, 2012), revisiting old battlegrounds to cast a footprint of the BHM known locally as *Batutut*. Dr. Jeffrey Meldrum deems the track a significant discovery.

▶ **Lost Tapes**, aired on Animal Planet between October 2008 and November 2010, took a wholly different approach to cryptozoology. While addressing well-known cryptids, it presented fictional vignettes in the style of films such as *The Blair Witch Project* (1999) and the *Paranormal Activity* franchise (2009-14), wherein "found footage" depicts events taped by participants, bystanders, or security cameras. None of the stories had any basis in fact, beyond longstanding reports of the cryptids involved. Bigfoot-related episodes included:

- "Bigfoot" (first aired October 30, 2008), wherein a poacher stalks forest ranger "Rachel Glen," menacing her life until Bigfoot arrives to save the day—and, incidentally, the local black bear population decimated by the rogue hunter.
- "Swamp Creature" (January 6, 2009), following university professor "Diane Chasny" and her nephew on an expedition to count alligators in Louisiana's Honey Island Swamp, harassed along the way by a resident humanoid creature.
- "Southern Sasquatch" (October 6, 2009), trailing three deer hunters from Fouke, Arkansas, to a deadly meeting with Miller County's "Boggy Creek" monster, leaving only one of the trio alive.
- "Devil Monkey" (October 12, 2010), in which "a young cousin of Bigfoot" savages law enforcement officers and moonshiners in the Appalachian Mountains of West Virginia.
- "Yeti" (October 12, 2010), wherein searchers seek the remains of "renowned billionaire explorer Mark Hordstrom," lost on Mount Everest in 2005, but find the Yeti instead, with predictably bloody results.

▶ **Finding Bigfoot**, premiering on Animal Planet in May 2011, adopted a serious documentary approach, following members of the Bigfoot Field Researchers Organization in pursuit of BHMs across the US and abroad. Team members include Matt Moneymaker, Cliff Barackman, James "Bobo" Fay, and Ranae Holland (a second-generation Bigfooter cast as the group's "lone skeptic"). The cast interviews eyewitnesses at various locales, then employs night-vision equipment, forward-looking infrared (FLIR) cameras, and call blasting to hunt their quarry. They have yet to catch a BHM, but many episodes produce strange nocturnal sounds that the team attributes to "Squatch." At press time, the show's episodes included:

- "Bigfoot Crossing in Georgia" (May 29, 2011), investigating a policeman's sighting and finding two possible footprints.
- "Swamp Ape" (June 5, 2011), tracking BHMs in northern Florida.
- "Caught on Tape" (June 12, 2011), pursuing evidence in North Carolina's Uwharrie National Forest, with squabbles over Moneymaker's leadership.
- "Fishing for Bigfoot in Oregon" (June 19, 2011), baiting Sasquatch with a rabbit, after hitting Ike's Pizza in Leaburg for "Bigfoot and Beer."
- "Frozen Bigfoot" (June 26, 2011), researching a mountaintop photo from Washington State and hearing nocturnal vocalizations.
- "Alaska's Bigfoot Island" (July 10, 2011), visiting the town of Hydaburg, where Bigfoot allegedly hurled a log at a passing taxi.
- "Behind the Search" (July 17, 2011), back to Leaburg for more suds and personal reflections on the quest, including unaired footage from prior episodes.
- "Birth of a Legend" (October 30, 2011), a Halloween special pilgrimage to Bluff Creek, California, joined by Bob Gimlin.
- "Baby Bigfoot" (January 1, 2012), launching the show's second season with scrutiny of the "New York Baby Footage" and uncovering new witnesses.
- "Big Rhodey" (January 8, 2012), reviewing a videotape of a purported BHM in Rhode Island.
- "Canadian Bigfoot, Eh?" (January 15, 2012), researching another video, this one from the Canadian Rockies.
- "Peeping Bigfoot" (January 22, 2012), turning to Minnesota with recorded howls and a report of an eleven-foot-tall BHM.
- "Buckeye Bigfoot" (January 29, 2012), penetrating Ohio to investigate another videotape.

Promotional advertisement for *Finding Bigfoot*. Pictured left to right: Cliff Barackman, James "Bobo" Fay, Ranae Holland, and Matt Moneymaker.
Credit: Author's collection.

- "Virginia is for Bigfoot Lovers" (February 12, 2012), wherein yet another video sends the cast in pursuit of the "Beast of Gum Hill."
- "Moonshine and Bigfoot" (February 19, 2012), with glowing eyes reported from Kentucky's Daniel Boone National Forest.
- "The Best of Finding Bigfoot" (February 26, 2012), a time-out retrospective replaying clips from prior episodes.
- "Hoosier Bigfoot" (March 4, 2012), in which a broad-daylight taping draws the team to Indiana.
- "Holy Cow, It's a Bigfoot" (March 11, 2012), following reports of a videotaped Bigfoot sighting in Utah.
- "Ripped From the Headlines" (November 11, 2012), kicking off season three with Dr. Jeff Meldrum and video evidence collected by Idaho high school students.
- "Untold Stories" (November 11, 2012), wherein cast members relate their personal Squatching experiences.
- "Mother Bigfoot" (November 18, 2012), in which a trail camera photo depicting an apparent female Sasquatch with her child prompts a hunt in Vermont.

- "CSI Bigfoot" (November 25, 2012), raising hopes of possible BHM evidence in Oklahoma.
- "The Sierra Spy" (December 2, 2012), placing the team in contact with Native American tribesmen in California's Sierra Nevada Mountains.
- "Dances With Bigfoot" (December 9, 2012), seeking Arizona's Mogollon Monster with aid from Apache guides.
- "Bigfoot and Wolverines" (December 16, 2012), in which a phone call from Northern Michigan leads cast members into "one their most successful night investigations ever."
- "Bobo Marks His Turf" (December 23, 2012), using a hot-air balloon to hunt Bigfoot among New Mexico's Jemez Mountains.
- "Australian Yowie" (December 30, 2012), a two-hour special following the cast Down Under, in search of Bigfoot's Aussie kin.
- "Squatch Spies" (January 6, 2013), employing new high-tech thermal equipment to stalk a nocturnal howler in Washington State.
- "Bacon for Bigfoot" (January 13, 2013), with pork used as bait, when a Louisiana mayor invites the team to hunt a lurking creature.
- "Bigfoot Merit Badge" (January 20, 2013), taking the cast to Colorado, viewing a possible Bigfoot film from 1962 and drawing Girl Scouts to the hunt.
- "Bigfoot Hoedown" (January 27, 2013), wherein backyard photos lead the team to West Virginia.
- "Badlands Bigfoot" (February 10, 2013), following the team to interview Lakota Sioux witnesses on South Dakota's Pine Ridge Indian Reservation.
- "Indonesia's Little Bigfoot" (February 17, 2013), another trip around the world, this time to hunt Orang Pendek on Sumatra.
- "More Untold Stories: Squatchers Without Borders" (February 17, 2013), airing more footage cut from preceding episodes, with "the inside scoop" on expeditions to Australia and Indonesia.
- "Peek-A-Boo Bigfoot" (February 24, 2013), investigating trail camera photos from Tennessee's Great Smoky Mountains.
- "Bigfoot and the Redhead" (March 3, 2013), in which a video clip and a packed town hall meeting steer the team to Pennsylvania's Allegheny National Forest, using whale sounds to tempt a reply from Bigfoot.
- "Bigfoot Loves Barbeque" (March 10, 2013), exploring Connecticut, after a mother videotaping her children at play catches an unexpected visitor.
- "Virgin Bigfoot" (March 17, 2013), examining Oregon's "London Trackway" footprints from 2012, while team members dangle from a precipice to watch for BHMs.
- "Bigfoot the Friendly Ghost" (March 24, 2013), with audio recordings from Illinois leading the BFRO to a graveyard.
- "Vietnam: The Heart of Squatchness" (March 31, 2013), visiting Southeast Asia in pursuit of creatures US soldiers once dubbed "Rock Apes."
- "Untold Stories: Behind the Squatch" (March 31, 2013), aired immediately following the Vietnam episode, providing more previously unseen footage and a glimpse of Bobo's private life.
- "Return to Boggy Creek" (November 10, 2013), launches season four with an investigation of the Fouke Monster in Arkansas.
- "Surf's Up, Sasquatch" (November 17, 2013), taking the team to Santa Cruz, California, and the Bigfoot Discovery Museum, with a tour of local BHM "hot spots."
- "Best Evidence Yet" (November 24, 2013), revisiting Florida to check out possible thermal footage of a Skunk Ape.

- ▶ "Kung-Fu Bigfoot" (December 1, 2013), drawing the cast to China in search of the Yeren.
- ▶ "Sketching Sasquatch" (December 8, 2013), call-blasting in the Sierra Nevadas after reviewing new audio recordings from Lake Tahoe.
- ▶ "Lonestar Squatch" (December 15, 2013), luring the cast to East Texas with more thermal footage of a possible Bigfoot.
- ▶ "Abominable Snowman" (December 29, 2013), another foreign expedition, this time to the monasteries and forests of Nepal.
- ▶ "Big Sky Bigfoot" (January 5, 2014), probing reported BHM activity around Bozeman, Montana, baiting BHMs with a deer decoy.
- ▶ "Bigfoot of Oz" (January 12, 2014), scouring waterways around Wichita, Kansas, on foot and from the air.
- ▶ "Super Yooper Sasquatch" (January 19, 2014), wherein reports of Bigfoot stalking witnesses draws the team to Michigan's Upper Peninsula.
- ▶ "South Jersey Sasquatch" (January 26, 2014), attempting to discover whether "Jersey Devil" sightings indicate Bigfoot's presence in the Garden State.
- ▶ "Coal Miner's Bigfoot" (February 9, 2014), another visit to West Virginia, inspired by recent audio recordings of vocalizations.
- ▶ "1, 2, 3, 4, I Declare a Squatch War" (February 16, 2014), involving a wager to decide if Oregon is "squatchier" than Washington State.
- ▶ "Bigfoot Call of the Wildman" (June 8, 2014), opens season five with another visit to Kentucky, inspecting recent tracks and chatting with a witness who recalls a childhood close encounter.
- ▶ "Squatters for Sasquatch" (June 15, 2014), in which a trail camera photo of a possible juvenile biped draws the team to Virginia.
- ▶ "Beast of the Bayou" (June 22, 2014), wherein more trail cam footage takes the crew back to Louisiana.
- ▶ "Squatching in a Winter Wonderland" (June 29, 2014), visiting Dr. Jeff Meldrum and reviewing a half-century of sightings from Washington State's Blue Mountains.
- ▶ "Live to Squatch Another Day" (July 6, 2014), drawing the team back to Oklahoma, where they use a cherry picker and music to search for Bigfoot.
- ▶ "Bama Bigfoot" (July 13, 2014), probing the forests around Sylacauga, Alabama's "Creepy Mountain," where thermal imaging suggests BHM activity.
- ▶ "Bobo's Backyard" (July 20, 2014), in which the team investigates photos snapped near Fay's home in Humboldt County, California.
- ▶ "Biggest Search Yet" (July 27, 2014), in which a search begins from the Four Corners Monument to sweep Arizona, Colorado, New Mexico, and Utah.
- ▶ "Squatching in the Midnight Sun" (November 9, 2014) launches season six with another trip to Alaska,, dividing the team between two target areas.
- ▶ "Untold Stories: Alaska Behind the Scenes" (November 9, 2014), a special bonus episode immediately following the one described above.
- ▶ "Baked Potato Bigfoot" (November 16, 2014), following the team to Idaho.
- ▶ "Squatchers Take New Jersey" (December 28, 2014), pursuing BHM reports from the Garden State.
- ▶ "British Bigfoot" (January 4, 2015), sending the team to the United Kingdom in search of elusive monsters.
- ▶ "Untold Stories: UK Behind the Scenes" (January 4, 2015), yet another follow-up episode, including outtakes and discussion of the show aired earlier.
- ▶ "Matt Goes Home" (January 11, 2015), wherein Matt Moneymaker leads the team over his home turf in Ohio, scene of his first personal sighting.

- ► **"Bigfoot Basecamp"** (January 18, 2015), in which the team visits Minnesota, investigating footprints found in March 2013.

- ► **"Paranormal Squatchtivity"** (January 25, 2015) draws the team back to Pennsylvania, prowling woods where both BHMs and ghosts have been reported.

► **Mountain Monsters**, premiering on Destination America in June 2012, follows a six-man group dubbed Appalachian Investigators of Mysterious Sightings (AIMS), led by founder "Trapper John" Tice, and does its best to imitate the faux backwoodsmen of *Duck Dynasty*, while pursuing cryptids through the Appalachian Mountains. Tice maintains the group's website, after a fashion, directing: "Please send all media request [*sic*] to Destination America's PR Department. Thanks You [*sic*]!" So far, only one episode—"Perry County Grassman," aired June 29, 2013—has dealt with a Bigfoot-type creature. Overwhelming negative reviews have not prevented the show's renewal for a second season.

Spike TV's *10 Million Dollar Bigfoot Bounty* completed its first season in 2014 without finding proof of Bigfoot's existence. Nine teams began the quest in January, with two pairs of finalists lurching through "36 Hours of Hell" on St. Valentine's Day. No one collected the $10 million, but contestants Dave and Stacy won a $100,000 research grant from Spike for their superior teamwork. Runners-up Kat and Michael bagged two DNA samples during the hunt, but both proved to be human.

"Messin' with Sasquatch™"

Rather surprisingly, TV's most entertaining Bigfoot is found in a series of commercials for Jack Link's® Beef Jerky, airing since 2006. The hilarious "Messin' with Sasquatch™" campaign, boasting production values higher than most modern Bigfoot fright films, pits human practical jokers against a Sasquatch who invariably treats them to some unpleasant surprise in return. In the "Snackin' with Sasquatch" ads, Bigfoot moves indoors—joining a women's book club, helping with car repairs, playing poker with friends—all equally delightful. If this is the closest you ever get to Bigfoot, it could certainly be worse!

Sasquatch as salesman extraordinaire for Jack Link's® Beef Jerky.

Credit: Jack Link's® Beef Jerky, used by permission.

Creature Features

BHMs have been a staple of horror films since the 1950s, including *The Snow Creature* (1954), *Man Beast* (1956), *The Abominable Snowman* (1957), and *Half Human* (1958). While those all featured Asia's Yeti, Bigfoot came into its own during the 1970s, riding the coattails of Roger Patterson's film. Documentaries vied for attention with low-budget horror films such as *Bigfoot* (1970), *Curse of Bigfoot* (1976), and *Revenge of Bigfoot* (1979). In the twenty-first century, directors have walked a line between chills and chuckles, sometimes stumbling on their way. The films produced by press time include:

▶ **Ape Canyon (2002)**, wherein a solitary Bigfoot—described by director Jon Olsen as "North America's Greatest Lover"—enriches the erotic life of bored waitress Darcy, until her jealous husband arrives with guns blazing.[1]

Poster for *Ape Canyon.* Credit: Author's collection.

▶ **Sasquatch (2002)**, filmed as *The Untold* and released in France as *Inexplicable*, comes billed as being "based on a true story." Lance Henriksen stars in his first Bigfoot feature as a businessman seeking his daughter, lost when her plane crashed on Squatch turf.

▶ **Among Us (2004)** follows B-movie director "Billy D'Amato" on a forest film shoot, where he meets a real-life monster and winds up fighting for his life.

▶ **Suburban Sasquatch (2004)** pits rangers and a Native American tracker against a kill-crazy BHM rampaging through suburban parkland. Part of the direct-to-video Decrepit Crypt of Nightmares series.

▶ **Sasquatch Hunters (2005)** is directed by Marc Messenger, who describes the film as "a mockumentary following a number of unusual characters as they search for, and obsess over, Bigfoot. We meet several groups: The Bigfoot Society, a cell of true believers; the American Hominid Association (AHA), a government funded band of trackers; and the Michigan Cryptozoological Institute, a cult-like organization devoted to welcoming the Sasquatch-American into western society."[2]

▶ **The Unknown (2005)**, also known as *Clawed*, opens with Bigfoot killing a group of poachers, then pits revenge-minded townsfolk against high school students bent on protecting the creature.

▶ **The Beast of Bray Road (2005)** is not a Bigfoot film, per se. Based very loosely on Linda Godfrey's first study of Wisconsin's "dogman," the film

Poster for *Clawed*, alternate title *The Unknown*. Credit: Author's collection.

veers into low budget horror with a slapstick twist, losing all contact with reality.

▸ The Lumberjack of All Trades (2006) mixes horror with strained comedy. Can an alcoholic logger and his misfit friends stop a savage Sasquatch from ravaging their small community? Who knows? More to the point, who cares?

▸ Legend of the Sandsquatch (2006) finds the titular monster terrorizing Sue and friends, as they search for missing Grandpa Frank.

▸ The Sasquatch Gang (2006) is described by writer/director Tim Skousen as follows: "Young fantasy/sci-fi aficionado Gavin Gore and his friends stumble onto some huge footprints in the woods. A local cop, reporter, and a renowned Sasquatch authority investigate, while two of Gavin's dim-witted neighbors hatch a scheme to profit from the situation."[3]

Poster for *The Sasquatch Gang*. Credit: Author's collection.

▸ Cryptid (2006) opens with the murders of South African farmers by a creature unknown to science. An international team of scientists arrives to investigate.

▸ Abominable (2006) is a low-budget pastiche of Alfred Hitchcock's *Rear Window*. Confined to a wheelchair by the auto accident that killed his wife, Preston Rogers watches in horror as a killer Bigfoot picks off his neighbors. Lance Henriksen logs his second Sasquatch outing as part of a civilian hunting party.

Poster for *Abominable*, lifting its basic plot from Alfred Hitchcock's *Rear Window*. Credit: Author's collection.

▸ Yeti: A Love Story (2006), written and directed by partners Adam Deyoe and Eric Gosselin, follows five college students on a camping expedition that goes awry with discovery of a savage gay Yeti and the cult that worships it.

▸ Bigfoot (2006), filmed in Ohio, is summarized thusly by writer/director/co-star Bog Gray: "In a place where man and nature have co-existed for years, man has finally overstepped his bounds and nature is fighting back."[4]

▸ Sasquatch Mountain (2006) features Lance Henriksen in his third Bigfoot feature, this time juggling sheriff's deputies and ruthless bank robbers while seeking revenge on the BHM responsible for his wife's death.

▸ Operation Nightscream 2003 (2007) is a documentary directed by

---

investigator John Freitas, including interviews with John Green and James "Bobo" Fay before he found fame on Finding Bigfoot.

▶ There's Something Out There (2007) was inspired by ferry operator Bobby Clarke's videotape of a possible Bigfoot, shot in April 2005 along Manitoba's Nelson River. As described by its producers, it "documents the weird and wild clash of cultures between the Hollywood interlopers and a small Northern community, and follows Bobby Clarke on his own personal journey into the mystery known as Sasquatch."[5]

▶ Southern Fried Bigfoot (2007), directed by Sean Whitley, explores Bigfoot sightings and legends in the American South. Zane Boyd dons the ape suit between interviews with witnesses and researchers, including Loren Coleman and Dr. John Bindernagel.

▶ Bigfoot Lives (2007), a documentary released a year before the Georgia Bigfoot hoax, follows "world famous Bigfoot hunter" Tom Biscardi and his team in search of evidence from New York to Montana.

Video cover for Bigfoot Lives, first in a series of Tom Biscardi documentaries. Credit: Author's collection.

▶ The Long Way Home: A Bigfoot Story (2007) won several awards at various second-string film festivals. A failed reporter on the skids returns to his small hometown to mend fences while Bigfoot prowls the neighborhood.

Writer/director James "Bubba" Cromer promises "an hysterical funny [sic], yet dramatic midnight movie that will not be forgotten for a long time after the 71 minutes it captures the viewer."[6]

▶ Blood Monkey (2007) is the first of twenty-four films in a series of Maneater movies produced for TV. It features one-time Oscar winner F. Murray Abraham fallen on hard times as an anthropologist seeking "missing links" in the jungles of Thailand.

▶ No Burgers for Bigfoot (2008) impressed reviewer Phil Hall as "a wonderfully sly deadpan comedy from Oklahoma filmmaker Jonathan Grant. Wearing five hats here (director, producer, writer, editor and star), Grant pulls off an amazing feat in skewering the pretensions and inanities of no-budget indie filmmaking in a manner that is thoroughly original and completely unpredictable." In Hall's words, the mockumentary "takes a cinéma vérité approach to how a very bad movie idea metastasizes into a thoroughly atrocious end product."[7]

▶ Prey for the Beast (2008) matches a group of weekend warriors and nubile hikers against a rampaging BHM, in a film Internet reviewer "Foywonder" deems "more gory than allegory."[8]

▶ The Shrieking (2008) offers up more college students who regret their plans for camping "as they stumble upon something in the woods that should not be."[9]

▶ Bigfoot: A Beast on the Run (2008) is a documentary including interviews with Tom Biscardi, M. K. Davis, Dr. Jeff Meldrum, Peggy Marx, Don Monroe ("The 'Indiana Jones' of Idaho"), and Thom Powell. Neal Burgstahler discusses photos of "Bigfoot orbs," offered as proof that BHMs travel between dimensions.[10]

▶ The Wildman of Kentucky: The Mystery of Panther Rock (2008) follows a fictional "Reality Team of

Special Investigators" to investigate Bigfoot reports around Lawrenceville, Kentucky.

▶ Not Your Typical Bigfoot Movie (2008) was described on a now-defunct website as "a documentary exploring the American Dream through the lives of Bigfoot researchers Dallas Gilbert and Wayne Burton in rural Appalachian Ohio." The hour-long film also makes time for Tom Biscardi.

Poster for *The Wildman of Kentucky: The Mystery of Panther Rock.* Credit: Author's collection.

▶ Hair of the Sasquatch (2008) is a comedy written by Rodger Cove, who also stars as "Rodger." Two filmmakers collide with reality while researching Bigfoot's legend from a marketing perspective.

▶ Strange Wilderness (2008) is a comedy, written and directed by Fred Wolf, that follows two TV stars to the Andes in a quest to jump-start ratings for their failing wilderness-themed program.

▶ The Wild Man of the Navidad (2008), written and directed by the team of Duane Graves and Justin Meeks, spins a horror tale around an actual BHM reported from the Navidad River bottoms of nineteenth-century Texas.

▶ Yeti (2008) is the thirteenth of twenty-four Maneater movies produced for TV since January 2007. Members of a college football team face frostbite and a spring-loaded Yeti

after their plane crashes in the Himalayas while en route to Japan. Why they didn't fly direct from the US across the Pacific is anyone's guess.

▶ Sawtooth (2009) warns us on its posters that "the truth does exist." Three outcast high school students find it, to their sorrow, while investigating rumored Bigfoot sightings near their hometown.

▶ Assault of the Sasquatch (2009) imagines what might happen if a bear poacher's arrest brought his latest quarry—a living, rapacious Bigfoot—into an urban setting. As the posters warn: "New Territory...Fresh Prey."

Poster for *Assault of the Sasquatch.* Credit: Author's collection.

▶ More Than Myth (2009) is a half-hour short film from writer/director/producer/star Levi Isaacs, casting himself as a teenager who learns the truth about Bigfoot from a wise park ranger.

▶ Bigfoot Is Real! Sasquatch to the Abominable Snowman (2010) is a documentary written by O. H. Krill, more familiar to moviegoers from his several films on UFOs.

▶ Monster in the Woods (2010) is a family affair, written and directed by Mike Stanley, starring Serena and Veronica Stanley as two of three girls who seek Bigfoot in the forest surrounding their hometown.

▶ The Bloody Rage of Bigfoot (2010) is

another family gathering, written and directed by James Baack, with Andrew and Bianca Baack in supporting roles. Bianca seduces and kidnaps "one of the world's leading experts on Sasquatch," with predictably gruesome results.[12]

▶ The Bigfoot Hunter: Still Searching (2011) follows two cryptozoologists and several other paranormal investigators on a BHM hunt in southern New York. Greg Newkirk directs the fictional tale.

Poster for *The Bigfoot Hunter: Still Searching*. Credit: Author's collection.

▶ Letters from the Big Man (2011) stars Lily Rabe as a government hydrologist surveying Oregon's Kalmiopsis Wilderness after a forest fire. She meets Bigfoot, and "as their friendship deepens, [she] must take bold steps to protect his privacy, as well as her own."[13]

Poster for *Letters from the Big Man*. Credit: Author's collection.

▶ Primitive (2011) brings star Matt O'Neill home to investigate his mother's slaying by a Bigfoot on a rampage.

▶ Dear God No! (2011) is a blood-soaked horror tale of outlaw bikers on the run, stopping at a disgraced anthropologist's Georgia cabin with a secret in the basement and a hungry monster in the woods outside.

Poster for *Dear God No!* Credit: Author's collection.

▶ Blood of Ohma (2011) offers a revenge plot, with "Jody Meyer" (Addison Kinnear) stalking the Bigfoot that slaughtered her parents years earlier. The cast boasts three other Kinnears, with writer Mark Cray in a supporting role.

▶ Bigfoot Lives 2 (2011) is Tom Biscardi's sequel to 2007's *Bigfoot Lives*. Stops along the way include Alabama, Florida, Kentucky, Louisiana, South Carolina, and Texas.

▶ Shriek of the Sasquatch! (2011), written and directed by Steve Sessions, veers back into low-budget horror, complete with simulated film damage, as young lovers Nick and Julie meet Bigfoot on a 1979 road trip.

▶ Anatomy of a Bigfoot Hoax (2011) displays near-unrivaled chutzpah, "exposing" the 2008 Georgia Bigfoot hoax courtesy of co-director and star Tom Biscardi. Viewers "witness the dissection of the 'Bigfoot Body' as the

Video cover for *Shriek of the Sasquatch*. Credit: Author's collection.

Searching for Bigfoot Team did in real time."[14] And if you buy that, have I got a Sasquatch for you!

▶ Snow Beast (2011) casts John (*Dukes of Hazard*) Schneider as a field researcher who links declining Canadian wildlife populations to a rogue Bigfoot. Panic ensues.

▶ Sweet Prudence & the Erotic Adventure of Bigfoot (2011), written and directed by William Burke, comes advertised as "a hilarious new film combining science fiction, comedy and erotica, all set against the pastoral splendor of an actual Nudist Resort!"[15]

▶ Bigfoot: The Lost Coast Tapes (2012) is another "found footage" movie, wherein a disgraced investigative journalist stakes his comeback and the lives of his film crew on debunking reports of a Bigfoot corpse.

Poster for *The Lost Coast Tapes*. Credit: Author's collection.

▶ 1313: Bigfoot Island (2012), "shot on location in Bigfoot country," tells the story of a woman who "summonds [*sic*] the mythical beast to right the wrongs inflicted on her."[16]

▶ Lost Woods (2012), written by Phillip Ellering and star Joey Brown, follows the degeneration of a camping trip into a trial by ordeal when Bigfoot drops by.

▶ Eaglewalk (2012), written and directed by Rob Himebaugh, is a thirty-minute film wherein Bigfoot raids a summer camp.

▶ Paper Dolls (2012) depicts another road trip gone wrong, as BHMs attack two friends in Montana's Glacier National Park.

▶ Night Claws (2012), written and directed by David A. Prior, pits a diverse cast of characters against another Bigfoot on a rampage.

Promotional advertisement for *Night Claws*. Credit: Author's collection.

▶ Bigfoot (2012) unites 1970s pop culture TV icons Danny Bonaduce and Barry Williams in a search for Sasquatch.

▶ The Movie Out Here (2012) follows a Toronto lawyer home to Fernie, British Columbia, for "a Western Canadian adventure, with Sasq sightings, bikini pillow fights, and of course, the Rangers."[17]

▶ Uwharrie (2012) is yet another "found footage" portrayal of Bigfoot terrorizing campers, this time in North Carolina. Director Christopher Flowers allows that the tapes "have yet to be authenticated."[18]

▶ The Legend of Grassman (2013) finds Ohio's Bigfoot turning the tables on monster hunters. Writer Dennis Meyer also stars, while brother Tyler directs.

▶ Exists (2013) provides more gore as Bigfoot disrupts a Texas woodlands party weekend.

▶ The Shadow of Bigfoot (2013) is a British entry to the list, written and directed by Philip Mearns. A Bigfoot hunter's reckless methods put his team at risk.

▶ Skookum (2013) revives Louisiana's long-dormant Beast of Bayou Dorcheat for a new killing spree.

Poster for *Skookum,* applying a Pacific Northwest aboriginal name to Louisiana's Bigfoot. Credit: Author's collection.

▶ American Sasquatch Hunters: Bigfoot in America (2013) traces the history of Bigfoot hunting from 1958 to present, including interviews with Dr. Jeffrey Meldrum, Stan Gordon, and world renowned primatologist Jane Goodall.

▶ Alien Paranormal: Bigfoot, UFOs and the Men in Black (2013) presents researcher Stan Gordon laying out the case for alien abductions and purported Bigfoot sightings linked to UFOs.

▶ Throwback (2013) sends gold prospectors into the wilds of Far North Queensland, Australia, where they run afoul of Yowie.

Poster for *Throwback.* Credit: Author's collection.

▶ Bigfoot Chronicles (2013), written by Thomas Nash Monson (who also stars), follows a skeptical filmmaker in search of BHMs. "Along the way he learns a lot about the illusive [*sic*] creature and in the process he finds himself."[19]

▶ Frostbite (2013) follows the travails of a schizophrenic teenager, traumatized by a Bigfoot hoax, who inherits a Finnish estate from his grandfather and meets the monster again on new turf, facing skepticism from locals.

▶ Abominable Snowman (2013), originally titled *Deadly Descent*, sends Brian Tanner to find out why his father disappeared on Glacier Peak, in Washington State, twenty years earlier. When he vanishes in turn, his sister takes up the search.

▶ Bigfoot Roadtrip (2013) follows the BFRO's Cliff Barackman from mountaintops and virgin forest to the Idaho State University laboratory of Dr. Jeff Meldrum.

▶ Dead Bigfoot: A True Story (2013) presents the "truth" about Justin Smeja's alleged Bigfoot kills in the Sierra Nevadas. Ro Sahebi directs and appears in the film, with Smeja and Bart Cutino. Bigfoot is conspicuously missing.

▶ Willow Creek (2013) is mockumentary written and directed by comedian-turned-filmmaker Bobcat Goldthwait. "Found footage" strikes again, when a

Bigfoot enthusiast and his skeptical girlfriend find horror waiting at the old Patterson film site.

Poster for Bobcat Goldthwait's *Willow Creek* mockumentary. Credit: Author's collection.

▸ **At the Dark Divide** is another Bigfoot film was announced in July 2013, but had not appeared by press time for *Seeking Bigfoot*. Rob Himebaugh planned a prequel to his short film *Eaglewalk* (see above), soliciting funds through Kickstarter online, with a goal of "making Bigfoot scary as hell."[20] The project's working title, *At the Dark Divide*, refers to the largest roadless area in western Washington State, 76,000 acres of wilderness between Mount Adams and Mount St. Helens, including fabled Ape Canyon (see Chapter 1).

▸ **Bigfoot Wars** (2014) is based on a series of popular horror novels penned by Eric S. Brown since 2011, this film starring Judd Nelson and C. Thomas Howell depicts carnage between Bigfoot and residents of a small American town.

▸ **Love in the Time of Monsters** (2014/15) is a "comedy horror film" directed by Matt Jackson, in which "[t]wo sisters travel to a cheesy tourist trap where they battle toxic monsters dressed in Bigfoot costumes in order to save the ones they love." Originally premiered in March 2014 at the Cinequest Film Festival, it failed to find a cinematic distributor, finally going direct to video in February 2015.

▸ **The Fiancé** (2015) is still "in production" as *Seeking Bigfoot* went to press, *The Fiancé* was promoted only on a dedicated website, which described it as follows: "When a beautiful bride-to-be is bitten by Bigfoot, she becomes a brutal force of nature hell-bent on breaking the engagement...and her fiancé!" This is not to be confused with a projected remake of a 1980 East German film by the same title, reportedly starring Oscar-winning actress Anne Hathaway.

Promotional advertisement for the forthcoming film *At the Dark Divide*. Credit: Author's collection.

"Don't Go in the Woods"

Lead singer/actor Jeff Sisson, drummer Chris Wilson, guitarist Jack Reidell, and bassist Ben VonSchiefelbusch comprise Troglodyte, a "death metal" band organized in 2005, in Kansas City, Missouri. Normally seen onstage in stylized ape or caveman masks, the group has released two Bigfoot-centric albums to date, both bearing "explicit lyrics" warnings.

Album cover for Troglodyte's *Welcome to Boggy Creek.* Credit: Author's collection.

Album cover for Troglodyte's *Don't Go in the Woods.* Credit: Author's collection.

Welcome to Boggy Creek (2011) includes the songs "Welcome," "Symphonie [*sic*] of Sasquatch," "Piece of You," "Mummified Yeti Hand," "Fight for Your Life," "Caught (On Super 8)," "Bring Me the Head of Bigfoot," "Beaten and Eaten," "Skunk Ape Rape: The Rapture," "They Walk Among Us," "Hit by the Hendersons," and "Fossil."

Don't Go in the Woods (2012) continues in the same vein, with "No Beast So Fierce," "Crippled Foot Cast," "Cro-Magnum Force," "The Trap is Set," "Red Handed," "Murderous Bi-Pedal Hominid Rampage (Where are My Legs?)," "Sasquatch Ocean," "In Search Of...," "Don't Go in the Woods," "Nowhere to Hide," "Minnesota Iceman Cometh," "Oregon Trail," and "352" [referring to the most famous frame of Roger Patterson's film].

While their music won't please everyone, Troglodyte's album covers stand as classics in the seedy Bigfoot-run-amok genre.

It seems certain Bigfoot will continue haunting movie theaters and TV screens, at least as long as it makes money for producers. Modern Americans appear to have an insatiable appetite for BHMs—as movie monsters do for human flesh." ☺

END
NOTES

▶ Introduction

1. BFRO, www.bfro.net/GDB/default. asp. Retrieved Jan. 9, 2014.

▶ Chapter 1

1. Old Oregon, www.oldoregonphotos. com/elkanah-walker-early-oregon-missionary-1871.html. Retrieved Jan. 9, 2014.
2. The E. Walker Letter, www.bigfoot-lives.com/html/e_walker.html. Retrieved Jan. 9, 2014.
3. Theodore Roosevelt, *The Wilderness Hunter* (New York: G. P. Putnam's Sons, 1893), p. 441-442.
4. Ibid., p. 443.
5. Ibid., p. 444.
6. Ibid.
7. Ibid., pp. 446-447.
8. John Green, *Sasquatch: The Apes Among Us* (North Vancouver, B.C.: Hancock House, 1978), pp. 103-104.
9. Ibid., pp. 110-111.
10. Police Magistrate A. M. Naismith affidavit, Aug. 20, 1957.
11. Fred Beck, *I Fought the Apemen of Mount St. Helens*, Wa. (Kelso, WA: The author, 1967), www. bigfootencounters.com/classics/ beck.htm. Retrieved Jan. 9, 2014.
12. Green, *Sasquatch*, p. 97.
13. Beck, *I Fought the Apemen*.
14. Ibid.
15. Michael Dennett, "The Rent [*sic*] Mullins Saga: Bigfoot Jokester Reveals Punch Line—Finally." *Skeptical Inquirer 7* (Fall 1982): 8-9.
16. Peter Byrne, *The Search for Bigfoot: Monster, Myth or Man?* (New York: Pocket Books, 1976), p. 2.
17. Ivan T. Sanderson, "A New Look at America's Mystery Giant." *True Magazine* (March 1960), www. bigfootencounters.com/classics/ ruby.htm. Retrieved Jan. 9, 2014.
18. Ibid.
19. Ibid.

20. Ivan T. Sanderson, *Abominable Snowmen: Legend Come to Life* (Philadelphia: Chilton Books, 1961), pp. 76-78.
21. Ibid.
22. Ibid.
23. Ibid., p. 79.
24. Ivan T. Sanderson, "The Strange Story of America's Abominable Snowman," *True Magazine* (December 1959), www. bigfootencounters.com/articles/ true1959.htm. Retrieved Jan. 9, 2014.
25. Ibid.
26. John Driscoll, "Birth of Bigfoot," *Eureka Times-Standard*, Oct. 30, 2008.
27. Sanderson, "The Strange Story of America's Abominable Snowman."
28. Driscoll, "Birth of Bigfoot."
29. Ibid.
30. Ibid.

Chapter 2

1. BFRO Report #36072.
2. Ibid., Report #26604.
3. Ibid., Report #27459.
4. Ibid., Report #28642.
5. Ibid., Report #36498.
6. Ibid., Report #39181.
7. Ibid., Report #35596.
8. Ibid., Report #7771.
9. Ibid., Report #40618.
10. Ibid., Report #30530.
11. Ibid., Report #29357.
12. Ibid., Report #40220.
13. Bigfoot: The Beast of Kentucky, http://bigfootlore.blogspot. com/2014/01/new-sighting-martinsville-indiana-01-16.html.
14. *New York Times*, Sept. 5, 1886.
15. BFRO, Report #35828. (According to the website, this sighting occurred on June 29, but was reported to BFRO on June 19, a physical impossibility. I have used the former date.)
16. Ibid., Report #38980.
17. Ibid., Report #13350.
18. Ibid., Report #27991.

19. Ibid., Report #36572.
20. Ibid., Report #13494.
21. Ibid., Report #41169.
22. Ibid., Report #19472.
23. Ibid., Report #17292 .
24. Ibid., Report #28702.
25. Ibid., Report #40381.
26. Ibid., Report #13285.
27. Ibid., Report #25484.
28. Ibid., Report #23732.
29. Ibid., Report #30906.
30. Ibid., Report #25265.
31. Ibid., Report #33336.
32. Ibid., Report #32537.
33. Ibid., Report #12562.
34. Ibid., Report #29455.
35. Rick Berry, *Bigfoot on the East Coast* (Stuarts Draft, VA: The author, 1993), p. 94.
36. BFRO, Report #34485.
37. Ibid., Report #28445.
38. Ibid., Report #34657.
39. Ibid., Report #30622.
40. Ibid., Report #26205.
41. Ibid., Report #22386.
42. Ibid., Report #34460.
43. Ibid., Report #29139.
44. Ibid., Report #26113.
45. Ibid., Report #12482,
46. Ibid., Report #39855.
47. Ibid., Report #12205.
48. Ibid., Report #41657.
49. Ibid., Report #40204.
50. Green, *Sasquatch*, p. 6.
51. BFRO, Report #23245.
52. Ibid., Report #12001.
53. Ibid., Report #35177.
54. Ibid., Report #24733.
55. Justin Nobel, "Nunavik hunters run into rock-throwing bigfoot creature," *Nunatsiaq News*, Oct. 25, 2013.
56. BFRO, Report #17221.

▶ Chapter 3

1. "John Willison Green," http://en.wikipedia.org/wiki/John_Willison_Green. Retrieved Jan. 23, 2014.
2. "Loren Coleman," http://en.wikipedia.org/wiki/Loren_Coleman. Retrieved Jan. 23, 2014.
3. Jerry Coleman, "Four Steps Toward Becoming a Cryptozoology Field Researcher," www.cryptozoology.com/blog/blog.php?id=46. Retrieved Jan. 23, 2014.
4. "Growing Up Coleman," www.cryptozoology.com/blog/blog.php?id=54. Retrieved Jan. 23, 2014.
5. "Strange Highways, Indeed," www.cryptomundo.com/cryptozoo-news/jdc. Retrieved Jan. 23, 2014.
6. Jesse Alderman, "Idaho professor's Bigfoot research criticized," *Seattle Times*, Nov. 3, 2006.
7. Brian Dunning, "Killing Bigfoot with Bad Science," http://skeptoid.com/episodes/4011. Retrieved Jan. 23, 2014.
8. "Top 100 Researchers/Figures in Bigfoot history," https://www.facebook.com/notes/bigfoot/top-100-researchersfigures-in-bigfoot-history-we-are-thankful-for-these-men-and-/179904168692905. Retrieved Jan. 23, 2014.
9. Ibid.
10. Amazon.com, www.amazon.com/Sasquatch-Rising-2013-Breakthroughs-Backyard/dp/1466360569/ref=pd_sim_b_3. Retrieved Jan. 23, 2014.
11. "In Search of the Alabama Bigfoot," www.gmdstudios.com/weblab/freakylinks/WWWFRE~1.COM/FREAKO~1/TAILS_~1/ALABAM~1.HTM. Retrieved Jan. 23, 2014.
12. West Coast Sasquatch Research, http://sasquatch-bc.com/jbinder.html. Retrieved Jan. 26, 2014.
13. "About Cliff," http://cliffbarackman.com/about. Retrieved Jan. 26, 2014.
14. Theo Stein, "Bigfoot Believers," *Denver Post*, Jan. 5, 2003.

15. Loren Coleman review of "Behind the Mysteries: Bigfoot," www.lorencoleman.com/behind_mysteries.html. Retrieved Jan. 26, 2014.
16. Austin (TX) *American-Statesman*, Oct. 4, 2009.
17. Mary Lee Grant, "Wrestling with Bigfoot," *Houston Press*, March 13, 2003.
18. GCBRO, http://gcbro.com/about.htm. Retrieved, Jan. 26, 2014.
19. Neil Arnold, "Interview with Bart Nunnelly," http://zooform.blogspot.com/2008/09/interview-with-bart-nunnelly.html. Retrieved Jan. 30, 2014.
20. Kentucky Bigfoot Researchers, www.kentuckybigfoot.com/about_us.htm. Retrieved Jan. 30, 2014.
21. Eric Spitznagel, "Everything's Bigfoot In Texas," *Vanity Fair*, Oct. 30, 2008.
22. "Craig Woolheater bio," www.cryptomundo.com/craigwoolheater. Retrieved Jan. 30, 2014.
23. NAWAC, About Us, http://woodape.org/index.php/about-us. Retrieved Jan. 30, 2014.
24. "Robert W. Morgan," www.xzonedirectory.com/morganr.html. Retrieved Jan. 30, 2014.
25. MABRC forum, www.mid-americabigfoot.com/forums/viewtopic.php?f=23&t=3470. Retrieved Jan. 30, 2014.
26. West Coast Sasquatch Research, http://sasquatch-bc.com/tsteenburg.html. Retrieved Jan. 30, 2014.
27. Ibid., http://sasquatch-bc.com/steenburginterview.html. Retrieved Jan. 30, 2014.
28. Skunk Ape Research Headquarters, www.atlasobscura.com/places/skunk-ape-research-headquarters. Retrieved Jan. 30, 2014.
29. Sasquatch Investigation of the Rockies, http://sasquatchinvestigations.org/bigfoot-research-team. Retrieved Jan. 30, 2014.
30. BFRO, Report #2928.
31. Ibid., Report #24265.
32. Paula Schleis, "Kent man still chasing Bigfoot," *Akron Beacon Journal*, Jan. 29, 2012.
33. The Bigfoot Forums, http://bigfootforums.com. Retrieved Feb. 9, 2014.
34. Thom Powell, A Book Review of "In the Spirit of Seatco," www.bigfootencounters.com/reviews/seatco.htm. Retrieved Feb. 9, 2014.
35. Henry J. Franzoni III, www.henryfranzoni.com/index.html. Retrieved Feb. 9, 2014.
36. About Steve Kulls, http://squatchdetective.wordpress.com/about. Retrieved Feb. 9, 2014.
37. Squatchdetective, http://squatchdetective.com. Retrieved Feb. 9, 2014.
38. Drew Dakessian, "Hillsdale's Sasquatch expert," *Portland Tribune*, June 1, 2013.
39. North America Bigfoot Search, www.nabigfootsearch.com/directors_message_1.html. Retrieved Feb. 9, 2014.
40. NABS, www.nabigfootsearch.com/Raywallace.html. Retrieved Feb. 9, 2014.
41. Ibid., www.nabigfootsearch.com/habituation.html. Retrieved Feb. 9, 2014.
42. Loren Coleman, "Green's Personal Statement: The Tennessee Bigfoot Affair," www.cryptomundo.com/cryptozoo-news/green-on-carter. Retrieved Feb. 9, 2014.
43. Lisa Shiels, *Backyard Bigfoot: The True Story of Stick Signs, UFOs, & the Sasquatch* (Linden, MI: Slipdown Mountain Publications), back cover.

44. Amazon.com, www.amazon.com/
Backyard-Bigfoot-Story-Stick-
Sasquatch/dp/0974655368.
Retrieved Feb. 9, 2014.

45. Ibid., www.amazon.com/Impossible-
Visits-Interactions-Sasquatch-
Habituation/dp/1436398517.
Retrieved Feb. 9, 2014.

46. Robert Lindsay, "The Bigfoot
'Habituators,'" http://robertlindsay.
wordpress.com/2011/04/06/
the-bigfoot-habituators. Retrieved
Feb. 9, 2014.

47. "Jeremy Wells responds," www.
cryptomundo.com/cryptozoo-
news/manimal-4. Retrieved Feb. 9,
2014.

48. Robert Lindsay, "The Bigfoot
'Habituators.'"

49. Jerry Coleman, "Cryptozoological
Field Research//4 Steps," www.
cryptozoology.com/blog/blog.
php?id=46. Retrieved Feb. 16, 2014.

50. Ibid.

51. Tuan C. Nguyen, "Scientist
developing drone to hunt for
'Bigfoot,'" www.smartplanet.com/
blog/bulletin/scientist-developing-
drone-to-hunt-for-
8216bigfoot/4835. Retrieved Feb.
16, 2014.

52. "Conferences, Symposiums & Other
Get-Togethers," http://
bigfootforums.com/index.php/
forum/26-conferences-
symposiums-other-get-togethers.
Retrieved Feb. 16, 2014.

▶ Chapter 4

1. 10 Million Dollar Bigfoot Bounty,
www.imdb.com/title/tt2490294/
plotsummary?ref_=tt_ov_pl.
Retrieved Feb. 23, 2014.

2. Natalia Reagan, http://
nataliareagan.com. Retrieved Feb.
23, 2014.

3. Marcello Truzzi, "On the
Extraordinary: An Attempt at
Clarification." Zetetic Scholar Vol. 1,
No. 1 (1978): 11.

4. Craig Hilavaty, "PETA Says No to
Bigfoot Hunting," Houston
Chronicle, Jan. 29, 2014.

5. A Guide to Bigfoot Hunting, www.
bigfoothunting.com/hunting/
bigfoot_guns.shtml. Retrieved Feb.
23, 2014.

6. Bigfoot Ordinance 1984-2, www.
skamaniacounty.org/ordinance/
Ord_1984-2.pdf. Retrieved Feb. 23,
2014.

7. Whatcom County Resolution No.
92-043, www.co.whatcom.wa.us/
council/1992/res/res1992-043.pdf.
Retrieved Feb. 23, 2014.

8. Loren Coleman, "Texas Says It Is
Legal To Kill Bigfoot," www.
cryptomundo.com/cryptozoo-
news/tx-legal. Retrieved Feb. 23,
2014.

9. It is illegal to shoot a Sasquatch in
New York State, www.
bigfootencounters.com. Retrieved
Feb. 23, 2014.

10. Bigfoot Shootings, www.
lawnflowersjerkyandbigfoots.com/
Pages/BigfootShootings.aspx.
Retrieved Feb. 23, 2014.

11. Robert Lindsay, "Why No Bigfoot
Bones and Bodies?" http://
robertlindsay.wordpress.
com/2011/05/04/why-no-bigfoot-
bones-and-bodies. Retrieved Feb.
23, 2014.

12. Ibid.

13. Ibid.

14. Ibid.

15. Ibid.

16. Ibid.

17. Ibid.

18. Ibid.

19. Ian Simmons, "The Abominable
Showman," Fortean Times 83
(October 1995): 34-37.

20. Ivan Sanderson, "The Missing
Link?" Argosy (May 1969): 23-31.

21. Ibid.

22. Ibid.

23. Frank Hansen, "I Killed The
Ape-Man Creature Of Whiteface,"
Saga (July 1970): 8-11, 55-60.

24. Ibid.
25. Simmons, "The Abominable Showman."
26. Andy Campbell, "Minnesota Iceman: Mysterious Frozen Creature From '60s Resurfaces At Museum," *Huffington Post*, June 28, 2013.
27. YouTube, www.youtube.com/watch?v=niLvytleTA8. Retrieved Feb. 27, 2014.
28. Craig Woolheater, "Bugs and the Texas Bigfoot Bodies," www.cryptomundo.com/bigfoot-report/bugs-tx-bf. Retrieved Feb. 27, 2014.
29. "The 'Siege' at Honobia," www.bfro.net/avevid/ouachita/siege-at-honobia.asp.
30. Robert Lindsay, "The Siege of Honobia," https://robertlindsay.wordpress.com/2011/05/04/the-siege-of-honobia. Retrieved Feb. 27, 2014.
31. Ibid.
32. James Hagenbruber, "Bigfoot back?" *Billings Gazette*, Oct. 29, 2001.
33. Ibid.
34. Loren Coleman, "Has a Skunk Ape Been Killed in TN?" www.lorencoleman.com/skunk_ape.html. Retrieved Feb. 27, 2014.
35. Ibid.
36. Godlike Productions, www.godlikeproductions.com/forum1/pg1. Retrieved Feb. 27, 2014.
37. Loren Coleman, "Rumor: Bigfoot Shot At Pine Ridge," www.cryptomundo.com/cryptozoo-news/prbigfootshot. Retrieved Feb. 27, 2014.
38. Robert Lindsay, "Why No Bigfoot Bones and Bodies?"
39. Loren Coleman, "Massacre Mania Continues," www.cryptomundo.com/cryptozoo-news/massacre-cont. Retrieved Feb. 27, 2014.
40. Ibid.
41. Robert Lindsay, "Chronology of the Recent Bigfoot Shooting Story," http://robertlindsay.wordpress.com/2011/07/05/chronology-of-the-recent-bigfoot-shooting-story. Retrieved Feb. 27, 2014.
42. Derek Randles, "Sierra shooting," www.olympicproject.com/id16.html. Retrieved Feb. 27, 2014.
43. Ibid.
44. Robert Lindsay, "Chronology of the Recent Bigfoot Shooting Story."
45. Joe Black, "Just the FACTS—Smeja/Cutino Flesh Sample Hoax," http://bf-field-journal.blogspot.com/2013/03/just-facts-smejacutino-flesh-sample-hoax.html. Retrieved Feb. 27, 2014.
46. Justin Smeja's Official Polygraph Examination Report, http://bigfootevidence.blogspot.com/2012/08/justin-smejas-official-polygraph.html. Retrieved Feb. 27, 2014.
47. "Ames: Separated Spy, Agent Lives," *Washington Post*, April 29, 1994.
48. Sharon Hill, "Altoona PA Bigfoot shooting rumor—Case closed," http://doubtfulnews.com/2013/05/altoona-pa-bigfoot-shooting-rumor-case-closed. Retrieved March 2, 2014.
49. "PBS: Summary Report on Alleged Pennsylvania Bigfoot Shooting Case 5-16-2013," http://bigfootevidence.blogspot.com/2013/05/pbs-summary-report-on-alleged.html. Retrieved March 2, 2014.
50. Ibid.
51. James Nye, "Was a Bigfoot shot and killed in rural Pennsylvania? Conspiracy theorists go wild with speculation after local resident's 911 call," *Daily Mail* (London), May 29, 2013.
52. Broadcastify, www.broadcastify.com.

53. "PBS: Summary Report on Alleged Pennsylvania Bigfoot Shooting Case 5-16-2013."

54. James Nye, "Was a Bigfoot shot and killed in rural Pennsylvania?"

55. Ibid.

▶ Chapter 5

1. List of tallest people, http:// en.wikipedia.org/wiki/List_of_ tallest_people. Retrieved March 15, 2014.

2. Loren Coleman, *Bigfoot! The True Story of Apes in America* (New York: Simon and Schuster, 2009), p. 127.

3. The Bossburg, Washington (Cripple) Tracks, www.bigfootencounters. com/articles/bossburg.htm. Retrieved March 21, 2014.

4. Grover Krantz, Bigfoot Sasquatch Evidence (Surrey, BC: Hancock House, 1999), p. 56.

5. John Napier, *Bigfoot: The Yeti and Sasquatch in Myth and Reality* (New York: E. P. Dutton, 1973), pp. 116-17.

6. The Bossburg, Washington (Cripple) Tracks.

7. Jeff Meldrum, *Sasquatch: Legend Meets Science* (New York: Forge Books, 2006), p. 237.

8. Coleman, Bigfoot! p. 130.

9. Medical Dictionary, http:// medical-dictionary. thefreedictionary.com/ dermal+ridges. Retrieved March 22, 2014.

10. Grover S. Krantz, "Anatomy and Dermatoglyphics of Three Sasquatch Footprints," *Cryptozoology* 2 (Winter 1983): 72-3.

11. Michael R. Dennett, "Bigfoot evidence: are these tracks real?" www.bigfootencounters.com/ articles/skeptical.htm. Retrieved March 22, 2014.

12. John Berry and Stephen Haylock, "The Sasquatch Foot Casts," Fingerprint World 11 (January 1985): 59-63.

13. Glenn Alford, "Idaho State University Researcher Coordinates Analysis of Body Imprint That May Belong to a Sasquatch," Idaho State University Press Release, Oct. 23, 2000.

14. Ibid.

15. Ibid.

16. Green Says Skookum Cast May Be Proof, www.bfro.net/news/ bodycast/green_statement.asp. Retrieved March 23, 2014.

17. Hoaxer Cliff Crook promoting Phony Photo, again, www.bfro.net/ REF/hoax.asp. Retrieved March 23, 2014.

18. Coleman, Bigfoot! p. 22.

19. Marc Hume, "Controversy Surrounds Skookum Sasquatch Cast," *National Post*, March 3, 2001.

20. See http://prettyhands.wordpress. com/big-hands-for-your-height-a- way-to-find-out for calculations of hand length as an expression of height. Retrieved on March 23, 2014.

21. David Claerr, "Bigfoot Handprint Discovered In Texas," http://voices. yahoo.com/bigfoot-handprint- discovered-texas-6604970. html?cat=58. Retrieved March 23, 2014.

22. David Claerr, "'Baby' Bigfoot Evidence—Cast Prints from a Sasquatch Toddler," http://voices. yahoo.com/baby-bigfoot-evidence- cast-prints-sasquatch-11342564. html. Retrieved March 23, 2014.

23. Ibid.

24. Native American Names for Bigfoot, www.sunstar-solutions.com/ NAbigfootnames.htm. Retrieved March 23, 2014.

25. Green, *Sasquatch: The Apes Among Us*, p. 336.

26. Other Forms of Bigfoot Evidence, www.bigfoot-lives.com/html/ other_forms_of_bigfoot_evidenc. html. Retrieved March 23, 2014.

27. John Bindernagel, *North America's Great Ape: The Sasquatch* (Courtenay, B.C.: Beachcomber Books, 1998), p. 179.

28. Matt Moneymaker, "Deer Kills and Bigfoot," www.bfro.net/avevid/mjm/deerkills.asp. Retrieved March 23, 2014.

29. Alyssa Newcomb, "Pennsylvania Man Says 'Bigfoot' Vandalized His Winnebago RV," http://abcnews.go.com/blogs/headlines/2012/10/pennsylvania-man-says-bigfoot-vandalized-his-winnebago-rv. Retrieved March 24, 2014.

30. Priscilla Mason, "Michigan Man Accuses Bigfoot Of Property Damage And Pizza Theft," http://bizarrenewsnetwork.com/michigan-man-accuses-bigfoot-of-property-damage-and-pizza-theft. Retrieved March 24, 2014.

31. Ibid.

32. Roosevelt, *The Wilderness Hunter*, p. 445.

33. Robert and Frances Guenette, *The Mysterious Monsters* (Los Angeles: Sun Classic Pictures, 1975), p. 96.

34. Grover Krantz, *Big Footprints: A Scientific Inquiry Into the Reality of Sasquatch* (Boulder, CO: Johnson Books, 1992), pp. 133-34.

35. The Copper Finch, www.etsy.com/shop/TheCopperFinch. Retrieved March 24, 2014.

36. Ivan Sanderson, "More Evidence That Bigfoot Exists," *Argosy* 29 (April 1968): 72-3.

37. Meldrum, *Sasquatch: Legend Meets Science*, p. 262.

38. Bigfoot DNA, Hair Analysis, www.bigfootencounters.com/biology/hair_analysis.htm. Retrieved March 25, 2014.

39. Ibid.

40. Sanderson, "More Evidence That Bigfoot Exists."

41. Joshua Blu Buhs, *Bigfoot: The Life and Times of a Legend* (Chicago: University of Chicago Press, 2010), pp. 105-7.

42. Peter Byrne, "Robert 'Bob' M. Titmus, Bigfoot Veteran Woodsman," www.bigfootencounters.com/stories/byrne_on_titmus.htm. Retrieved March 25, 2014.

43. Guy Edwards, "Today in Bigfoot History: July 2, 1995: John Green Calls Peter Byrne a Fraud," www.bigfootlunchclub.com/2013/07/today-in-bigfoot-history-july-2-1995.html. Retrieved March 25, 2014.

44. Fiona Macrae, "The single hair that could FINALLY prove the Yeti really exists," *Daily Mail*, Aug. 1, 2008.

45. DT: Bhutan Yeti (Part 2), www.skepticalviewer.com/2009/11/07/destination-truth-bhutan-yeti-part-2. Retrieved March 25, 2014.

46. Ibid.

47. BBB Business Review, www.bbb.org/east-texas/business-reviews/laboratories-medical/dna-diagnostics-in-timpson-tx-24003140. Retrieved March 25, 2014.

48. Dmitri Bayanov, *In the Footsteps of the Russian Snowman* (Moscow: Crypto-Logos, 1996), pp. 46-52.

49. Sharon Hill, "The story of 'Zana,' wild woman, has been solved through DNA analysis," http://doubtfulnews.com/2013/11/the-story-of-zana-wild-woman-has-been-solved-through-dna-analysis. Retrieved March 27, 2014.

50. "Yeti Hair Defies DNA Analysis," *China Daily*, June 26, 2001.

51. Colleen Curry, "Bigfoot, Yeti Hair Samples Requested for DNA Analysis at Oxford," http://abcnews.go.com/blogs/technology/2012/05/bigfoot-yeti-hair-samples-requested-for-dna-analysis-at-oxford. Retrieved March 27, 2014.

52. Guy Edwards, "Cliff Barackman Expands on Hair Sample from *Finding Bigfoot* Oklahoma Episode," www.bigfootlunchclub.com/2012/11/cliff-barackman-expands-on-hair-sample.html. Retrieved March 27, 2014.

53. Sasquatch Genome Project, http://sasquatchgenomeproject.org. Retrieved March 27, 2014.

54. M. S. Ketchum, P. W. Wojtkiewicz, A. B. Watts, D. W. Spence, A. K. Holzenburg, D. G. Toler, T. M. Prychitko, F. Zhang, R. Shoulders, and R. Smith, "Novel North American Hominins, Next Generation Sequencing of Three Whole Genomes and Associated Studies," *DeNovo Journal of Science* 1 (Feb. 13, 2013): 1.

55. Matt Moneymaker on Sasquatch DNA Project, http://cryptomundo.com/bigfoot-report/mm-sasquatch-dna-project. Retrieved March 27, 2014.

56. Bigfoot/Sasquatch/Hairy Man DNA, www.nabigfootsearch.com/bigfoot_dna.html. Retrieved March 27, 2014.

57. Tim Fasano, "David Paulides lies about Bigfoot DNA study," http://bigfootevidence101.blogspot.com/2013/01/david-paulides-lies-about-bigfoot-dna.html. Retrieved March 27, 2014.

58. Sasquatch Genome Project.

59. Ibid.

60. Ibid.; Kerry Cook and Aliece Watts—Replaced Texas Forensic Science Commissioners, www.youtube.com/watch?v=VfHBBhlDrVw. Retrieved March 27, 2014.

61. Federal Bureau of Investigation, www.fbi.gov/about-us/lab/forensic-science-communications/fsc/july2006/research/2006_07_research01.htm. Retrieved March 27, 2014.

62. Andreas Holzenburg, www.bio.tamu.edu/FACMENU/FACULTY/HolzenburgA.php. Retrieved March 27, 2014.

63. Dr. Douglas G. Toler, MD, www.healthgrades.com/physician/dr-douglas-toler-2cyd4. Retrieved March 27, 2014.

64. Sasquatch Genome Project.

65. *DeNovo*—Special Edition, http://denovojournal.com/denovo_002.htm. Retrieved March 27, 2014.

66. Sasquatch Genome Project.

67. Ketchum Bigfoot DNA paper released: Problems with questionable publication, http://doubtfulnews.com/2013/02/ketchum-bigfoot-dna-paper-released-problems-with-questionable-publication. Retrieved March 27, 2014.

68. Ibid.

69. Ibid.

70. Bigfoot DNA Study Update—David H. Swenson, Ph.D. Biochemist Supports Study, http://bf-field-journal.blogspot.com/2013/02/dna-study-update-david-h-swenson-phd.html. Retrieved March 27, 2014.

71. Greenresourcesredux.com, http://ww1.greenresourcesredux.com. Retrieved March 27, 2014.

72. *DeNovo*—Special Edition.

73. Ketchum Bigfoot DNA paper released: Problems with questionable publication.

74. Drama Building For Bigfoot DNA, www.ghosttheory.com/2013/09/03/drama-building-for-bigfoot-dna. Retrieved March 27, 2014.

75. Russell Goldman, Geneticist Unravels Yeti's DNA," *ABC News*, Oct. 17, 2013.

76. Ibid.

▶ Chapter 6

1. Ami Angelowicz, "Randy Lee Tenley, The Man Killed In The Bigfoot Hoax, Incites Ethical Debate," www.thefrisky.com/2012-08-29/randy-lee-tenley-the-man-killed-in-the-bigfoot-hoax-incites-ethical-debate. Retrieved March 2, 2014.
2. Mark Nelson, "***BIGFOOT!!!***," www.angelfire.com/realm3/marknelson. Retrieved March 2, 2014.
3. John Freitas, "Newly Hoaxed Bigfoot Film—Separating Fact from Fiction," www.bigfootencounters.com/hoaxes/sonoma_footage.htm. Retrieved March 2, 2014.
4. Ibid.
5. Loren Coleman, "$17 Million For Baby Bigfoot," www.cryptomundo.com/cryptozoo-news/17-million. Retrieved March 2, 2014.
6. Ibid.
7. Ibid.
8. Ibid.
9. Ibid.
10. Ibid.
11. Ibid.
12. Loren Coleman, "Ultimate GA Bigfoot Hoax Timeline: 2008," www.cryptomundo.com/cryptozoo-news/hoax-tl-08. Retrieved March 3. 2014.
13. Loren Coleman, "Tom Biscardi: 35 Years Ago," http://cryptomundo.com/cryptotourism/biscardi-35. Retrieved March 3, 2014.
14. Loren Coleman, "The Ultimate GA Bigfoot Hoax Timeline," www.cryptomundo.com/cryptozoo-news/ultimate-timeline. Retrieved March 3, 2014.
15. Ibid.
16. Ibid.; Searching for Bigfoot, www.searchingforbigfoot.com. Retrieved March 3, 2014.
17. Loren Coleman, "The Ultimate GA Bigfoot Hoax Timeline."
18. Ker Than, "Bigfoot Discovery Declared a Hoax," http://news.nationalgeographic.com/news/2008/08/080818-bigfoot-dna.html. Retrieved March 3, 2014.
19. Loren Coleman, "Ultimate GA Bigfoot Hoax Timeline: 2008."
20. Minnow Films, www.minnowfilms.co.uk. Retrieved March 3, 2014.
21. Ibid., www.minnowfilms.co.uk/in-production/Shooting_Bigfoot.html.
22. Frank Cali, "Rick Dyer Announces There is a Live Bigfoot in Captivity," http://bigfootevidence101.blogspot.com/2013/08/rick-dyer-announces-there-is-live.html. Retrieved March 3, 2014.
23. "Buy 'After the Shot' and See Bigfoot in Person," http://bigfootevidence101.blogspot.com/2013/09/buy-after-shot-see-bigfoot-in-person.html. Retrieved March 3, 2014.
24. "Bigfoot body: Arizona tour canceled," www.kpho.com/story/24657934/bigfoot-body-on-display-in-phoenix-area. Retrieved March 3, 2014.
25. Ibid.

▶ Chapter 8

1. *Ape Canyon*, www.imdb.com/title/tt0398696/?ref_=fn_tt_ tt_1. Retrieved March 9, 2014.
2. *Sasquatch Hunters*, www.imdb.com/title/tt0197851. Retrieved March 9, 2014.
3. *The Sasquatch Gang*, www.imdb.com/title/tt0460925. Retrieved March 10, 2014.
4. *Bigfoot*, www.imdb.com/title/tt0834897. Retrieved March 10, 2014.
5. *There's Something Out There*, www.farpointfilms.com/ portfolio/18/there_s_something_out_there.aspx. Retrieved March 10, 2014.
6. *The Long Way Home: A Bigfoot Story*, www.imdb.com/title/ tt1247678/synopsis?ref_=ttt_ov_pl. Retrieved March 10, 2014.
7. *No Burgers for Bigfoot,* www.filmthreat.com/reviews/11161. Retrieved March 10, 2014.
8. *Prey for the Beast*, www.dreadcentral.com/reviews/prey-beast-2008#axzz2vYyoxGtR. Retrieved March 10, 2014.
9. *The Shrieking*, www.imdb.com/title/tt0456005. Retrieved March 10, 2014.
10. *Bigfoot: A Beast on the Run*, www.imdb.com/title/tt1340420. Retrieved March 11, 2014.
11. *Not Your Typical Bigfoot Movie*, cached on Google at http:// webcache.googleusercontent.com/search?q=cache:DKQLcck LaEsJ:notyourtypicalbigfootmovie. com/+&cd=1&hl=en&ct=clnk&gl=us&client=firefox-a.
12. *The Bloody Rage of Bigfoot*, www.imdb.com/title/ tt1734121/?ref_=fn_al_tt_1. Retrieved March 11, 2014.
13. *Letters from the Big Man*, www.imdb.com/title/ tt1783331/?ref_=fn_al_tt_1. Retrieved March 11, 2014.
14. *Anatomy of a Bigfoot Hoax*, www.imdb.com/title/tt1964489. Retrieved March 11, 2014.
15. *Sweet Prudence & the Erotic Adventure of Bigfoot*, www. sweetprudence.com. Retrieved March 11, 2014.
16. *1313: Bigfoot Island*, www.imdb.com/title/tt2083123. Retrieved March 11, 2014.
17. *The Movie Out Here*, www.imdb.com/title/tt2498626. Retrieved March 11, 2014.
18. *Uwharrie*, www.imdb.com/title/tt2334966. Retrieved March 11, 2014.
19. *Bigfoot Chronicles*, www.imdb.com/title/ tt3158728/?ref_=fn_al_tt_1. Retrieved March 12, 2014.
20. "At The Dark Divide Plans To Make Bigfoot Scary As Hell," www.youwoncannes.com/2013/07/08/at-the-dark-divide-plans-to-make-bigfoot-scary-as-hell. Retrieved March 12, 2014.

KEEP ON
'SQUATCH'N

About the Author

Seeking Bigfoot is **Michael Newton's** twelfth book in the field of cryptozoology.